PREHISTORIC AMERICA

PREHISTORIC

AMERICA

———————— ★ ————————

by ANNE TERRY WHITE

Illustrated by ALDREN WATSON

Landmark
BOOKS

RANDOM HOUSE · NEW YORK

CONTENTS

PREHISTORIC AMERICA

CHAPTER 1

Peter Dobson Looks at a Boulder

HIGH UP ON MT. TOM IN WESTERN MASSA-
chusetts there is a curious stone. It is a big granite boulder resting on a ledge of rock and looking for all the world as though some giant had
picked it up and set it there. Anyone can see
that the boulder doesn't belong to the mountain. For the ledge on which it rests is made of a

different kind of rock. That boulder was plucked from some other spot. It was transported to this place. It is as much a visitor on Mt. Tom as the boys and girls who clamber up to picnic and get a bird's-eye-view of the checkerboard fields and farms below.

But giants big enough to carry such a stone exist only in story books. So how actually did the granite boulder get up on Mt. Tom? And for the matter of that, how did all the other "transported boulders" that dot the northern part of the United States down to about the level of New York City get there?

There they are, some of them big as a house and weighing thousands of tons. There they are, perched on ledges of a different rock. Sometimes when the boulder is of some peculiar stone, you can even trace the place from which it came. It might be ten or twenty miles away. It might be at a lower level, too, proving that the boulder had actually been carried up hill!

What a riddle!

To be sure, if you had lived in the days before our American Revolution, the boulders wouldn't have puzzled you long. The nearest

4

natural scientist could have given you the answer. The boulders had got there by way of Noah's Flood. The Great Waters in which every living creature drowned except the beasts and the birds and the people in the Ark had tossed the rocks up there.

"Just imagine," the naturalist would have told you, "waves twenty times as high as any you ever saw. Imagine them traveling twenty times as fast. Think what strength such waves would have."

If you still looked doubtful and said you didn't believe even waves so big and fast could carry thousands of tons of rock up hill or wash halfway across a continent, the naturalist would have said, "Well, then imagine still bigger waves. Imagine them a hundred times as big."

It was very convenient having Noah's Flood to fall back on. Noah's Flood could be blamed for lots of things. It could be blamed for stony New England, for instance. All those millions and millions of stones which New England farmers had taken out of their fields and piled up into fences around their pastures and corn fields had been left there by the Flood. If you didn't want

5

to believe that, what other explanation could you suggest?

One man did suggest something else.

Peter Dobson of Connecticut wasn't a scientist. He was just a cotton manufacturer who could put two and two together and make it four. One day he stood watching his men digging a cellar for a new factory. With their picks the men were busily engaged getting great boulders out of the clay and hauling them off.

Peter Dobson examined first one boulder and then another. Something peculiar about the rocks struck him—all the boulders were really very much alike. They were all scratched and grooved and polished. And like the "transported boulders" on the mountain sides, each was worn smooth underneath. The boulders looked as if they had been dragged across the country over rocks and gravelly earth in one steady position.

"This can't be the work of waves," Peter Dobson thought, "not even if they were *mountain* high. All this scratching and grinding must have been done by ice. Once upon a time these rocks must have been frozen fast into an iceberg and dragged over the land."

When Peter Dobson told his idea to the scientists, a lot of them were interested. It seemed a very likely notion indeed. It was at any rate a good deal better than the theory that Noah's Flood had carried the rocks. Ice could definitely do things that waves could not.

The only trouble with the iceberg theory was that it couldn't account for all the facts. There simply were too many boulders. The clay in which the stones are found stretches like a belt all the way across northern United States. In some places that belt is five to twenty feet thick, in some places it piles up to two hundred feet.

What a lot of remarkable icebergs it would have taken to account for all those acres and acres, those miles on endless miles of boulder clay!

But if icebergs were not responsible, what was?

Every natural scientist in the world was puzzling over the riddle. Sooner or later somebody would hit upon the right answer.

And at last somebody did.

CHAPTER 2

Adventure on a Glacier

SWITZERLAND IS DOTTED WITH TRANS-
ported boulders just like New England. In that
country, too, nearly everyone had blamed the
huge stones on Noah's Flood. The one exception
was a simple mountaineer who, climbing often
high up where glaciers lie, saw things the scientists had failed to notice.

He held that glaciers were to blame. The reason he thought so was that he could see stones exactly like the valley boulders frozen into the glaciers right now. The same, slowly moving masses of ice, he believed, that were now high up on the mountains had at one time extended much farther into the Swiss valleys. Those glaciers had carried the boulders down with them. They had melted and left the rocks behind.

Now ideas once expressed are like electric sparks. They can set other men's minds on fire.

One day in the year 1836 a young Swiss college professor, Louis Agassiz by name, went visiting a friend of his. The two men had much in common. Agassiz was a professional scientist studying fishes. Charpentier was an amateur scientist studying anything in Nature that came his way.

It happened that Charpentier had heard the mountaineer tell his ideas about boulders. Charpentier had gone to see for himself, and the more he saw, the more convinced he became that the mountaineer was right. The minute Agassiz arrived, Charpentier started to talk glaciers and boulders and gravel.

"I'll take you where you will see the evidence

for yourself," he said enthusiastically. "I know you will be convinced."

"Nonsense," his friend answered. "Glaciers don't come down so far. Their place is high up on the mountains. That's where they are now and that's where they always must have been. It's too warm for glaciers down here."

But the idea of hiking and exploring was tempting in itself.

Not long after they set out, Agassiz was ready to take back everything he had said. His friend was absolutely right. Water could never have carried the huge boulders or laid down ridges of gravel in such a way.

"The trouble with you, Charpentier," Agassiz began to complain, "is that you are too timid. You don't go far enough in your thinking."

By the end of the summer he was saying, "You lack imagination, Charpentier. It is my opinion that all this region—not only Switzerland but most of Europe—was once covered by glaciers. In fact, I believe that a great ice cap, bigger than the one lying over Greenland today, once completely buried this part of the world."

Agassiz was convinced, but to himself he

11

added, "If I want to convince others, I've really got to study glaciers. I've got to learn what makes glaciers move and how they travel."

Whenever Louis Agassiz was studying anything, that thing became the most important thing in the world. Now it was glaciers. He had a hut built out on a huge block of stone caught in the middle of a glacier. A blanket served for a door. A hole under another boulder became a storehouse for food. Agassiz got guides to help and invited friends to share his adventure. Dragging a load of instruments, they arrived.

They had an auger to bore holes through the ice. They had thermometers to lower into the holes to see how cold the glacier was at this depth and at that. They had instruments to survey the position of eighteen big boulders which they meant to watch year after year to see how fast the glacier moved.

It had taken a lot of imagination to see Noah's Flood as the answer to the boulders. But people found it harder still to believe the story Agassiz had to tell when his adventure on the glacier was over. The idea of an ice cap thousands of feet thick was so new and strange. People were used to thinking of climate as always having been pretty much the way they knew it. In this place it was cold and in that place it was hot, here there was a desert and there everlasting snow. It was frightening to imagine Europe under a vast mantle of ice.

At first scientists refused to believe it. But one by one they had to give in. The proof was there— in the boulders, in the gravel ridges, in the way the living glaciers behaved.

And America? What had been the story there? In 1846 Agassiz came over to find out. He came because the King of Prussia was so delighted with the Ice Age theory that he had given Agassiz money for travel. Besides, the people of Boston had asked him to come and talk to them. But most of all Agassiz came because the boulders and gravel ridges were calling to him to read their story.

And he did. Agassiz looked at the boulders and the ridges and a vision of the past came before him.

He saw the summers year by year getting colder, the winters getting longer. The snow piled in ever greater and greater drifts. He saw the drifts turning to ice underneath. He saw the ice growing, moving, spreading out. He saw it picking up gravel as it went along. He saw it freezing around rocks and in the cracks of the rocks. He saw it plucking out huge chunks of rock and carrying them along over the mountains and down—wherever it went.

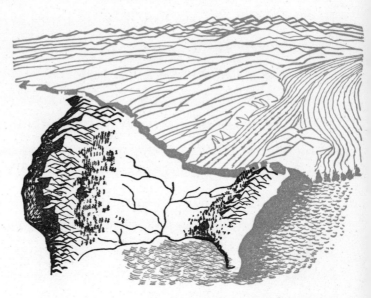

He saw the ice getting thicker and thicker—a mile thick, two miles thick. He saw Canada and Labrador and all the northern part of the United States buried under a huge cap of ice.

He saw the gravel-laden ice rasping like a saw

over bedrock. He saw it planing the rocks of New York and Minnesota and most of the States between. He saw it pressing so heavily in spots that great sections of the earth sank beneath the weight. He saw ice gouging out great U-shaped valleys. Over all the northern part of the United States lay the silence of death.

Then he saw the glaciers melting at their lower edges. He saw them dropping three million square miles of rock rubbish. He saw them leaving behind low gentle hills of earth which they had carried all the way from Canada to make the fertile lands of Iowa and Illinois. He saw the hollow places where the weight had been heaviest filling with water to make the Great Lakes. He saw a thousand gouged-out basins in Minnesota, Michigan, New Hampshire, and New York filling up with sparkling ice water.

All this had surely happened. But when?

Agassiz couldn't say. One thing he did know, however—it had all happened very slowly. He had studied glaciers long enough to know that they move only a few feet a year. So it must have taken the ice tens of thousands of years to come and tens of thousands of years to go.

What a shock that was to most people! They had grown up believing that the earth was created less than six thousand years ago—in the year 4004 B.C. Now there was this Ice Age. They would have to leave a lot of room on the calendar for that. All their neat little ideas of time would have to go out the window.

But the public had no notion what it was in for. Scientists had just begun to read the book of the earth. A lot more shocks were just around the corner.

CHAPTER 3

Down the Colorado

"WHEN?"

"How long ago?"

These two questions plagued every geologist who was poking among the rocks, studying the earth.

How could a person tell how old the earth was? For the matter of that, how could he tell how old any particular rock was?

One thing every geologist did know—not all

the rocks had been made in the same way. Some, it was clear, had come boiling up from inside the earth. Others had been made out of grains of sand or mud laid down by water. They knew that because there were sea shells in some of the rocks, and sea shells could mean just one thing— the sea. The sea had once been here. These rocks were a sea bottom turned to stone. The sea bottom had been pushed up.

When had this happened? How long ago?

Sometimes the geologists found rocks laid down by water in a neat formation, layer on top of layer, like the layers of a cake. They knew then that the lowest layer was older than the ones on top. They knew that the top layer was the youngest of the group. But how old was any one layer? And how many layers were there altogether?

The trouble with the earth was that its story was dreadfully mixed up. It would have been a lot easier to read if the layers had stretched like an onion skin all the way around the earth. But it wasn't that way at all. The story of the earth was different in different places. The same thing had by no means happened all over the earth at the same time.

Still, it would be very nice if you could cut straight down through all the layers at any one spot. Then you could at least read page by page—layer by layer, that is—all that had happened in that one spot. What a story it would be!

Now America was lucky. . . .

Far out west in Wyoming and Arizona, Colorado and Utah, Nature had done the very thing geologists were dreaming of. A river had cut its way straight down through more than a mile of rock layers. The sad part of it was that this open book of the earth's story was very difficult to get to and very dangerous to explore. Not until the year 1869 did anyone have the courage to try to read it.

The brave person was John Wesley Powell, a major of the Civil War who had lost an arm at the Battle of Shiloh. Afterwards Powell had become a college professor. He liked to take his students exploring. They would climb mountains, "oh" and "ah" over the scenery, and collect interesting bits of rock.

One day Powell and his boys camped near a trading post. It happened that Jack Sumner, the man who was running the trading post, had also fought in the Civil War. So it didn't take long for the two men to get together.

Powell told Sumner that he wanted to visit the Badlands. He didn't dare go alone, he said, because the unfriendly Sioux Indians were there.

"But if you come along as a guide," he added, "we could make it all right."

Sumner was disgusted. "Not me," he said. "I wouldn't waste my time messing around the Badlands. They're just plain stale. Everybody and his brother has been there. Now you listen to me. Why don't we do some real honest-to-goodness exploring? Let's you and me go down the Colorado River. Not even Indians have been down there."

Powell was taken aback. Down the unknown Colorado! It was as good as inviting death. There might be waterfalls along the stream. A person might easily be swept over and dashed to pieces on the rocks.

But all the time he was saying this, he was making up his mind to go. In the spring of 1869 the adventure started.

There were nine of them—Powell, his brother, Jack Sumner, and six more rip-roaring Westerners. Four sturdy boats stood ready to carry them and all their gear. They had guns, ammunition, instruments. They had food enough to last ten months.

"In case of accident," explained Powell. "Or if ice holds us up."

A group of trappers who had come to see them off stood grimly by. They shook their heads as they watched the party stow away their goods. "They ain't never coming back," they said. They laid bets that none of the nine would ever be seen again.

But Powell was confident. There was no reason, he felt, why they should not come out of the adventure alive. Anyhow, so far as waterfalls were concerned, they were in no danger. He was sure of that. Now that he had thought it through, he believed there couldn't be any falls in the Colorado. It was a very muddy river. It had carried so much sand for so many years that long ago it must have worn down the rocks in its channel to a point where there couldn't be any sheer drop.

Powell was staking the lives of nine men on this reasoning. And time proved his reasoning right. In all the 900 miles of their journey there were no waterfalls. There were rapids. The men did have spills. They did lose their tempers along with much of their food and gear. Bad luck so wore them down that three of the men finally left —only to be killed by Indians.

Even the Major thought of giving up. Had it not been for Johnny Hawkins, the brave young cook, Powell would have quit. But when Johnny said he'd go on alone, it was too much for Powell. He gritted his teeth. He held on till they reached the mouth of the Grand Canyon, which was as far as he was interested in going. Of the nine who started out, only Sumner and Hawkins reached the river's mouth.

Was the trip worth all the trials and dangers?

Every geologist living would answer "yes." For out of that trip came a new vision of America. Out of that trip came a new understanding of Time.

Many people since Powell have stood on the rim of the Grand Canyon and looked first out and then down. They have seen a chasm, a giant gully, stretching as far as the eye can see. That chasm is a mile deep. It is more than ten miles wide. It is three hundred miles long.

In the wall of this great chasm appear the cut edges of layer upon layer of rock. The hard rocks stand up like walls. The soft rocks have crumbled and make a slope. The whole looks like gaily colored sheets of cardboard laid one on top of another. Some sheets are red, some green, some gray, some white. Down at the very bottom of the gorge are the oldest rocks of all.

Powell saw all this. He saw it from the top down. He viewed it intimately ledge by ledge. He saw it from the bottom up. But he did much more. He understood the meaning of what he saw.

That narrow silver ribbon threading its way a mile below had once flowed at the top. Like a giant saw the river had cut its way through all the layers of rock above. Wind and rain and frost had done the rest. They had bitten into the sides of the canyon. The frost had cracked the rocks. The rain had dissolved the chemicals out of them. The rocks had decayed and crumbled and been swept down and washed away.

Slowly, slowly the canyon had been made. Grain by grain the work had been done. Yet enough rock had been taken away to make a mountain range 200 miles long.

What a job for stream and frost and rain and wind to do! And yet Powell knew that this was but a small part of the wearing away that had been done on this spot. When he examined the oldest rocks deep down in the canyon, he had seen that they were very different from the cardboard layers above. These rocks were tilted—they stood on end. There were cracks in them, too, and the cracks were filled with another kind of rock. Powell recognized that he was looking at the roots of mountains. Mountains higher than all the layers the Colorado had cut through had once been here.

Where had the mountains gone? How had they disappeared?

They had gone where all the rest had gone. They had been beaten down by the enemy. They had been worn away. Slowly, slowly frost and rain and wind had leveled them to a plain.

But even this was not all. Between the roots of the mountains that were gone and the next layer above, Powell found another wonder. There were remains of several layers that had been laid right on top of the mountain roots. Those layers had almost entirely disappeared. Yet Powell judged that they had been very thick. Perhaps they had been as much as 12,000 feet thick. That was twice the height of all the layers above the Colorado now. And all this, except a few traces, had been swept away.

Yes, much more had happened here than anyone except himself supposed. The Grand Canyon was only one of many scenes upon this spot.

Here, on this small piece of America, a great play had been acted. Mountains had risen out of the sea. Rain and frost and wind had chiseled the mountains into peak and ridge and valley. Then they had worn peak and ridge and valley to a plain. And again a sea had rolled over all. Powell saw no sign of a beginning. He saw no prospect of an end. This act had been repeated over and over again. It would go on and on.

How should he measure the play in years?

Suppose it took the Colorado a million years to get through the mile of rock. How long then did it take to form the rock itself?

Powell gazed down into the deepest depths. He tried to estimate how old those lowest rocks were. He could not make up his mind. But this he was sure of—he was looking into the dim ages that had been before there was any life on earth. Taken all in all, two thousand million years would not be too great an age for those earliest rocks.

How privileged he was to see all this! He understood America now as no other human being had done. People spoke of everlasting hills. That was only because men's lives were so short—they could not see the hills being worn down. But mountains could not stand forever, mountains were not a permanent part of the scenery. America was a land of constant change. Her mountains and her rivers and her lakes, her plateaus and her plains had come and gone, come and gone. All the mountains in America were young—the old mountains were all gone. . . .

What new ideas all these were! It would take a while to get used to them. It had been hard enough after Agassiz, who made people think of Time in tens of thousands of years. Now thousands must give way to millions. Compared with the rocks down in the bottom of the Grand Canyon, the Ice Age was just the other day.

Yes, the Ice Age was just yesterday.

CHAPTER 4

Marsh Does Some Digging

AFTER POWELL, THINGS WERE NEVER THE same again. Every day, it seemed, the earth scientists came out with something new. Now the talk was all about "fossils." You couldn't seem to buy a newspaper that didn't have some story about "fossils" in it. Generally it was about somebody in Kentucky or Connecticut or Missouri

28

or some other place who had found a "new fossil". It might be a bone or a tooth, or a shell, or even just a piece of wood that had turned to stone—petrified wood, they called it. If you asked a scientist why so much fuss was being made about such worthless things, he would look at you in shocked surprise.

"Worthless!" he would say. "Don't you understand? These are not just ordinary bones and teeth and shells and twigs of trees. They are pieces of animals and plants that lived and died long ages ago. They tell us what things were like in America millions and millions of years ago. They tell us what the country looked like, what kind of climate it had, what kind of creatures lived in it."

And he would go on to repeat a lot of the things Powell had just finished saying.

He would tell you: "You mustn't think America was always the way it is now. America is a land of constant change. Our mountains have come and gone, come and gone. The Sierra Nevadas and the Rockies are quite new. Moreover, much of what is now land was once upon a time a shallow sea. The sea came and went, came and went

—twenty times, perhaps. Sometimes that sea was bigger than all Europe. Sometimes America looked like a lot of islands sticking out of the water. Once three-fifths of America went under."

You had to believe him. He had the proofs. He could take you to a museum and show you fossil corals and snails that had come out of rock quarries near Chicago. He could show you shells of clams from rocks just outside Minneapolis. He could show you sponges that had come from Iowa farmlands. The sea had been in all these places.

You would go home thinking about these things. And next time you saw something about fossils in the paper, you read the story to the end.

Around the year 1870 the fossil news got very exciting. Out in the Western prairies a man named Othniel Marsh was finding some very curious bones.

Marsh was a professor from Yale. He was out in the prairies with a lot of his students and Buffalo Bill, who was acting as their guide. They were hunting fossils for a new museum. Marsh's rich uncle, Peabody, had given the museum to Yale, and Marsh himself was doing his best to fill it with the best bones in America. Mr. Peabody had left his nephew $100,000, too. Marsh thought the best thing to do with his money was buy bones.

Now very few people would choose to spend a fortune that way. But it was as natural for Marsh to be a fossil hunter as for an acorn to become an oak.

When he was a boy, Marsh had lived only a mile from the Erie Canal. It had just been built then. The rock rubbish was lying around in heaps, and the boy naturally poked around in it. The fossils in the rock fascinated him. Some he found looked very much like horseshoe crabs. Scientists called them trilobites. The trilobite, they said, was one of the very oldest creatures of the sea. It had lived about half a billion years ago. The shallow sea that had covered this region had been its home. There was no Lake Erie then.

After this the boy had kept a careful eye out for fossils. The biggest event of his 'teens was when he found two pieces of backbone in a coal bed up in Nova Scotia. The bones, he decided, belonged to an ancient halibut. But Agassiz, who was the world's fossil fish expert, said "no"; the bones were much more important. They had belonged to some unknown animal that had been fifteen feet long. The animal had lived in the water. It was neither fish nor reptile, but something in between.

How could Othniel Marsh want to be anything but a fossil hunter after that?

Marsh studied fossils at Yale. He studied them in Europe. He brought two and a half tons of bones back with him to America. America, he decided, was 'way behind Europe in fossils, and it would be his business to put it 'way ahead.

Now most of the finds in America had been made in Kentucky. But Marsh wanted to do his fossil hunting in the West. Kansas, Nebraska, the Dakotas, Colorado, Utah, Wyoming, Montana—these, he knew, were once the bottom of a sea. He had a notion that this old sea bottom would prove to be a fossil hunter's paradise.

And now in 1870 the newspapers were beginning to scream that it was so. Marsh was sending mountains of rock from the West and the rock was full of bones. The bones were all jumbled together. They were like huge jig-saw puzzles. But the scientists at Yale were putting the puzzles together. The animals they reconstructed out of the bones were strange and wonderful. They were different from any animals living anywhere in the world.

Marsh was having a splendid time. There seemed to be no end to the surprises. America was a country that had never stood still for long. Every few million years the scenery had changed, and the animals had changed along with it.

One day he had a bigger surprise than usual. He was digging in the side of a dried-up river bank in Kansas. The river bank was made of chalk—it had been formed a hundred million years ago. Sticking out of the chalk Marsh saw a small but very unusual looking bone. It was about six inches long, one inch wide, and hollow. Its walls seemed to be no thicker than a piece of blotting paper. Marsh thought it looked like a bird bone. But he had studied bones long enough to know that no bird could use one quite like that. He chipped it out very carefully. What was it?

It seemed to him he had seen only one bone

that closely resembled this one. That was the finger wing bone of a flying dragon. Had there been dragons in America as well as Europe?

The bone was important, it was very important. That he knew. Marsh wrapped it up with great care and took it to New Haven to study. He looked through all the bone books he had brought back from Europe. There was nothing else the bone could be—it must be a flying reptile's.

In his mind's eye Marsh saw the creature whose finger bone this had been. It was huge, but it wasn't heavy. With its bones hollow and so thin, it couldn't have weighed much over twenty-five pounds. The reptile had no teeth, Marsh decided, and it had fed on fish. It had had a wing span of twenty feet. Perhaps it was the greatest flying creature the world had ever seen.

People grew thoughtful when they read about Marsh's winged dragon, Pteranodon. They recalled the fairy stories they had read about flying dragons and brave youths who rescued beautiful maidens. Was it possible? More bones were proving that Marsh was right.

"What next?" Americans wondered.

Next was a story of birds with teeth. Again it came from the Kansas chalk. And again it made front-page news. For who had ever heard of a bird with teeth? Didn't people joke about it and say, "as rare as hen's teeth?"

But it was absolutely true. Marsh's birds from the Kansas chalk definitely had teeth. In other respects his smaller birds were pretty much like the sea gulls everybody knew. But his big bird was really rare. It was five feet from beak to toe tip and it had ninety-four sharp teeth in its mouth. Marsh called it Hesperornis—Western Bird.

35

Western Bird was a diver. He was a swimmer. But he couldn't do much else. He couldn't fly because he had no wings—just a tiny bone where wings generally are. And he couldn't walk much because his great strong feet were not built for land. They stuck out like a pair of paddles at right angles from his body and looked as if they couldn't be set down to walk on at all.

"Did this creature big as a man get around on land by wriggling?" people wondered.

But they didn't stop to wonder long—their attention jumped to a still more amazing fossil. Hesperornis had been hero for a day. Now Marsh's Great and Terrible Lizard was crowding him off the front page.

CHAPTER 5

The Great and Terrible Lizard

As a matter of fact, he wasn't marsh's
lizard. Marsh wasn't doing any digging himself
now. He had decided he would get more done if
he stayed quietly in New Haven and let other
collectors send their fossils to him. Word had
got around that Marsh paid fancy prices for

bones. And that's how the Great and Terrible Lizard came into his hands.

One day in 1877 a school teacher named Lakes was hunting for fossil plants out in Colorado. Near the town of Morrison he stumbled across six feet of bone. It was a backbone.

"Maybe," he thought, "this will interest that Yale professor."

So Lakes made a sketch of the bone and sent it to New Haven. Then he collected a ton or more of other fossils in the area and sent them off to New Haven, too.

Lakes fully expected the professor would come rushing out to make a deal with him. But Marsh was busy opening his museum. Time passed. Lakes got tired. If Marsh didn't want the bones, Lakes knew somebody else who would. He packed up a second lot and sent them to Edward Cope, another scholar and fossil collector.

Marsh went wild when he heard of it. For by this time he had looked the fossils over and recognized that they were very special. They were the bones of a monster that had measured at least sixty feet in length and had stood twenty feet high!

There was not time to be lost. If he was to get the best and biggest bones for his museum, he must tie up Lakes right away. He wired one of his paid collectors in Kansas to rush out to Morrison. "Buy every fossil Lakes has," he ordered. Above all, the collector was to try and get back the bones Lakes had sent to Cope.

Now Cope had every intention of buying the bones himself. But he was so busy talking about them and writing about them that he hadn't got around to paying for them. He was just getting ready to publish an article about the bones when Lakes wired him to turn the fossils over to Marsh.

Cope wasn't going to take this lying down. That Yale professor had stolen a march on him. But this wasn't the end. He, Cope, was a scholar, too. He had money like Marsh. He was just as stubborn a fighter. He'd show Marsh a thing or two.

So there was a battle. Or, rather, there was a war. For the two men fought and quarreled over the bones of the Great and Terrible Lizard and his relatives for years.

And while they fought, every man, woman,

and child in America got acquainted with a new word—dinosaurs.

Dinosaurs, they learned, had been the biggest beasts that ever walked the earth. Just before the Rockies were born, they had been kings in Wyoming, Colorado, Montana. For a few million years they had stomped around, terrifying every living thing. Then they had disappeared. Not anywhere in the world was there a dinosaur left. The closest things to them were crocodiles and birds.

The papers obligingly carried sketches of the beasts. Every time a new fossil came out of the rocks, the public was treated to his picture.

Some dinosaurs had walked on two feet. Some had walked on four. Some had gone in for armor plate. Some had favored horns. One had a neck twenty feet long. Others had boasted tails weighing any number of tons.

But it was one thing to see a picture in the paper. It was another to see the skeleton itself. When Marsh got his Thunder Lizard set up in the museum, people by the thousand poured in to gape at him. It was a proud moment for Marsh. Brontosaurus had cost him $30,000.

Marsh thought he was worth every penny of it.

There stood the giant who for millions of years had been buried in stone. There he stood on his four elephantine legs. His long neck supported a ridiculously small head. His huge tail stretched on and on behind him. He was sixteen feet high. He was sixty-seven feet long. His bones weighed six tons and a half. The earth had trembled when he passed.

He looked so terrible. People had a hard time believing that Brontosaurus had been a mild and placid creature who minded his own business. But Marsh insisted it was so.

"Look at his teeth," Marsh said.

And, indeed, the teeth backed him up. Brontosaurus was not a meat eater. His teeth had all they could do to cut the stems of the plants he fed upon. He had slushed around in the swamp that was his home and put all his mind on getting enough to eat. It had taken a lot of fodder to keep his forty tons of flesh and bone going.

People stood and gaped at Brontosaurus. To think such creatures had once tramped around America! This one, at least, had been a peaceful fellow. But some of those others! That twenty-five-foot one from Colorado, for instance, the one with the three-horned bone helmet. He was always looking for a scrap. And the one with the huge armor plates on his back. That was something to meet on a dark night!

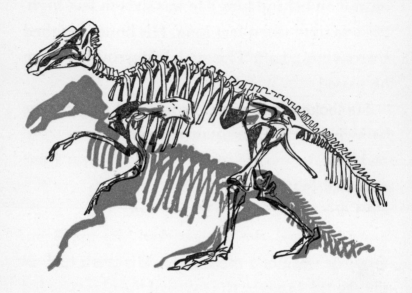

Now the scientists were talking about still another fellow, the biggest nightmare of them all. He had stalked around on his hind legs, they said. He was forty-seven feet long and stood eighteen or twenty feet high. And his teeth and claws were something wicked. He scrapped, they said, with anything that came in sight and made a meal off it. He had made life miserable for the vegetable-eating lizards, who just couldn't bite back.

People stood and gaped at the Great and Terrible Lizard.

Why had he passed out of the world? Was it because the climate changed? Was it because the great swamps disappeared? Was it because there wasn't enough green stuff left for dinosaurs to eat?

Nobody had the answer. All the professors could say was that the dinosaurs were gone. Like the great Western Bird, like the Winged Dragon, they had had their day.

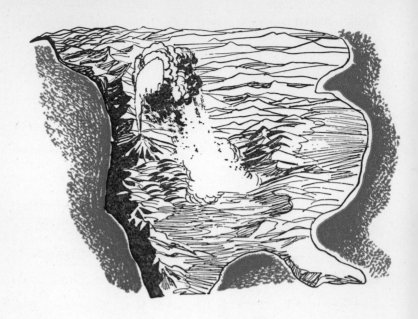

CHAPTER 6

Quicksand of the Niobrara

BRONTOSAURUS KEPT DRAWING THE crowds. People said he was better than anything P. T. Barnum, the circus man, had to show. In thousands of homes the Thunder Lizard made table talk at breakfast, dinner, supper, luncheon.

One thing about the creature puzzled folk.

44

Brontosaurus had been taken out of the rock. But how had he got into the rock in the first place?

This was something to which the scientists themselves had only recently got the answer. Not that the right answer hadn't been given long ago. It had. The ancient Greek philosophers knew it. The Italian painter, sculptor, architect, engineer Leonardo da Vinci knew it. But it wasn't convenient to hear the right answer. It didn't fit in with a lot of other things people had been taught. So they put it out of their minds. It was easier all around if you said the fossils were "freaks of nature."

Or you could put the blame on Noah's Flood. That was safe, too. You could say the shells had been washed up by the Flood and afterwards buried by the sand and mud it left behind. As for bones and teeth, they had belonged, you could say, to drowned sinners—the little ones to dwarfs, the big ones to giants.

That's how the Governor of New York explained the big tooth dug up in 1706. It was almost six inches long and weighed two and a quarter pounds. The Governor got quite excited

45

and wrote to Cotton Mather, the famous Puritan preacher, about it.

"I am perfectly of the opinion," he said, "that it was a human tooth." The giant, he said, had doubtless "waded as long as he could keep his head above the clouds." But at last he had been drowned with all other creatures.

The scientists knew better now. They had the answer so pat that they could even guess where the good digging places would be. There was one good rule. To find fossil bones it was best to go where water had been.

"You can easily see why," the scientists would say. "If an animal dies on dry land, its bones don't have much chance to be preserved. Look at what happened to the bones of the millions of buffalo who died on our prairies. They are all gone. Summer sun and winter frost and snow don't take long to turn bones into dust. Besides, meat-eating animals get hold of bones and destroy them. Roots of plants, too, find their way into cracks and break the bones up. A bone has lots of enemies.

"No, if bones are going to become fossils, they've got to be covered up from the air right away. A creature that dies where its body will be swept into the sea has a good chance to become a fossil. But it must be swept far out. If it isn't, the waves will pound it to pieces on the shore. Or sea worms will get into the bones.

"An animal that sinks in a quiet lake has a good chance to become a fossil. So has one that lands in a quiet bay. In such places mud and sand will soon cover up the bones. More and more will pile on top. The lime in the water will cement the mud and sand into a solid mass. The mass will turn to stone. And the bones will turn to stone with it."

Then the scientists would go on to say that the surest way for an animal to become a fossil was to fall into a quicksand. And they would begin to tell you about James Cook.

James Cook was a frontier scout and a big game hunter out in Wyoming. The two things kept him pretty busy. But there were days in the 1870's when he found better ways of spending his time. He had a sweetheart in Nebraska and thought nothing of riding three or four hundred miles on horseback to see her. Her father owned a cattle ranch on the Niobrara River.

One summer day the two young people were riding over the range together. They had gone about three miles from the ranch house when they came to two high, cone-shaped hills. The hills looked tempting.

"Let's climb up," said Cook. "There's bound to be a fine view from the top."

So they dismounted. They let the reins of their bridles drag on the ground as a sign to the horses to keep close and started to climb.

Now about halfway up the steep side they noticed a strange thing—the hillside was covered with pieces of bone. Where on earth had the bones come from? Cook looked up at the rock ledges above.

"It might be," he said, "that long ago an Indian brave was buried here under a ledge of rock. I've heard tell that Indians used to kill ponies and bury them near the bodies of their braves. These might be the ponies' bones."

Just then his eye caught a glitter inside one of the pieces. He stooped and picked it up. It was a leg bone. The marrow hole was filled with tiny crystals. The bone had turned to stone.

Suddenly James Cook remembered something. He thought of a stone tooth that Chief Red Cloud of the Sioux had once showed him. The Chief had been talking to him about "stone bones." Afterwards Red Cloud had told a story about some Indians of long ago.

A group of them, he said, had once been faced with starvation. But the Great Spirit had not let them die that slow and painful death. He had sent a "thunder horse" and the "thunder horse" had killed them all instantly. To prove his story, Red Cloud had brought out the stone tooth. It had measured four inches across.

James Cook had no idea what the real story of that stone tooth was. But somehow he couldn't help connecting it with the bone in his hand. Was this bone also out of the long ago?

For years the stone bones on the hill continued to haunt him. Long after he had married and bought his father-in-law's ranch, he kept thinking about them. The hills were always there reminding him. And the papers nowadays were full of tales about fossils. Perhaps these bones were important. Perhaps he ought to tell the scientists about them.

At last he decided to get them off his conscience. And then such strange things happened that James Cook could only shake his head over it all.

Who would have dreamed that the whole hill was filled with bones? Who would have thought there could be so many bones in *any* one place? Group after group of scientists had come. They had dug and chipped and chipped and dug and still there seemed to be no end to them.

Out of one hill alone the scientists had taken so many bones that Cook had lost count of them. The scientists kept a count, though. They said 3,400,000 bones had been taken out—enough to make up 17,000 skeletons. How many there were in the other hill they wouldn't even guess. Likely there were bones enough there for all the museums in the world.

He, James Cook, had thought that first fossil bone belonged to a pony. And now rhinoceroses were walking out of his hill! True, they were only about the size of a great hog, but they were rhinoceroses just the same—with two horns side by side on their noses. And in what unbelievable numbers! Out of 17,000 skeletons, 16,000 were rhinos.

When he hunted he had seen buffalo by the thousand. He had seen pronghorn antelope in vast herds. Now in his mind's eye James Cook saw the rhinoceroses that had trampled the Nebraska plains some thirty million years ago. He saw the animals quietly browsing. He saw them wary, snorting, pawing the ground with angry feet, stampeding.

And with them he could see a second strange animal which the scientists were putting together from the bones. *Moropus* they called the creature. They made a quick sketch of him for the ranchman. "See," they said, "*Moropus* was a little of this and a little of that. His head and neck were like a horse's. His body went like this— thick and sloping like a tapir's. His legs were stocky like a rhino's, but longer. His teeth were like those of no living creature at all. And on his feet this grazing creature had great claws instead of hoofs. What the claws were for we can't imagine."

James Cook took the scientists' word for the beasts. He had a lot of respect for the men who were unscrambling the bones. He would ride out to the quarries and watch the digging. He liked to hear the scientists talk. They would chip away and talk and he would watch and listen. And while he listened, slowly the valley he knew would fade out of sight and he would catch a glimpse of a world 30,000,000 years ago.

The earth was having one of its warm spells then. Greenland was really a green land, covered with oaks and evergreens. Forests of palms grew in central Europe, camphor and cinnamon, too. All over the Rockies and up into Montana great forests spread. Irises and roses bloomed where only sage and bunch grass grew today.

But not all of America was a pleasant land There were dry places where the wind blew hard. It lifted the sand and filled the air with it. Then woe to every creature there. Sometimes herds of browsing animals would sense the storm coming. They would huddle together for protection. And the cutting, flying sand would bury them there where they stood.

Then there were broad plains where almost nothing grew. Herb-eating animals who wandered there had a hard time of it. And when there was a dry spell, things were very bad indeed. The herds would seek water and not find it. They would go panting, staggering across the plains. Then perhaps they would see water ahead. Mad with thirst they would rush towards it. They would throw themselves into the ponds or rivers. They would trample each other under foot. And sometimes that water hid a treacherous quicksand. The thirst-crazed animals would rush in, not knowing. They would be caught in the shifting sands and sucked down. Seeking to save their lives, they would lose them.

Surely this was the secret of the hills. Surely

this was what had happened here on his ranch on the Niobrara. Today the hills were high above the river. Yesterday they were a quicksand under it.

James Cook, frontier scout, big game hunter and ranchman, stood and watched the digging. He listened to the talk. What a feeling of time it gave you to know the secret of the hills! It was something you couldn't rightly express.

CHAPTER 7

The Great American Play

MAJOR POWELL HAD SAID, "AMERICA IS a land of constant change." And now a great many people were really getting to believe it. How could they help it when newspapers and magazines kept breaking out with pictures of animals no one had ever heard of?

People got the feeling, as they read, that they

were watching a great play. The scientists had divided the play up into acts. In each act—or "age," as the scientists called them—different plants and animals took the leading parts. Sometimes a character that had a quite unimportant part in one age became the hero of the next. And in the following age it might be a minor character again. It might even go off the stage altogether and never come back.

The scientists said there was something mysterious about the way the play started.

"We can't be sure," they said, "that the beginning really *was* the beginning. You see, there are no fossils in the oldest rocks. But that does not necessarily mean there were no living creatures then. The answer more likely is that creatures living in those earliest times simply left no traces behind them.

"You see," the scientist explained, "it's the hard parts of a creature that generally become fossils. If a creature has no hard parts, it isn't easy for it to leave a record. So there might have been life and yet we would have nothing to show for it. Life might have gone on for a thousand million years before there was a single fossil."

Anyway, there it was. When the curtain went up, a good many characters were already on the stage. And certainly they acted very much at home. They weren't very big, as animals go. But they filled the shallow seas of America. Trilobites, sponges, corals, sea worms, snails, clams —each was there in a lot of different varieties.

Yet in one way all of them were alike—not one of them had a backbone. Instead, nearly all the creatures had gone in for armor. Shells, shells, shells. The creatures boasted shells of a hundred different kinds. And inside each shell a soft, moist little animal was spending its life trying to get enough to eat.

The creatures were small, as animals go. They were simple. And they weren't very bright. Yet for a hundred million years they held the stage alone. They kept the play going. They crawled and burrowed and waved to and fro. They hid in the seaweed and grew shells. Then some of them made their bow and left the stage for good.

A new act opened. A new set of actors took the stage. Most of the spineless creatures were still around, but fishes were stealing the show from them. The fishes had surprising talents—they could swish their tails and be off somewhere else before you knew it. They could flap their fins and shoot off in a different direction. They could cover a lot of sea in a day looking for food. Also they had teeth to capture their food with and make short work of it afterwards.

Definitely fishes were a success. A thousand different kinds roamed the shallow seas of America. They swam around and ate what they could get and laid their eggs and fought one another. It was their act, their age—the Age of Fishes.

Anybody could see that the new creatures were built on a superior plan. They had a skeleton *in*side their bodies. They had muscles on the *out*side. The muscles were attached to the skeleton and could move it. That meant greater speed. It also meant a sort of safety. With the skeleton on the inside there was less chance of its getting broken.

The earliest fishes didn't feel it was protection enough. It was all very well having the skeleton safe inside. But what about the muscle? It would never do to leave it right where other fish could bite into it.

So they had a coat of horny armor. The armor was as clumsy as the armor of some of the knights. The knights could hardly move around when they got their iron on. And the fishes were loaded down with their armor, too. Some of them were so weighted down they had to lie and wait for prey to come close to their noses. Huge armored fishes lay low on the sandy bottom of the sea that covered northern Ohio. They lay and waited. Their open jaws were terrifying. The mouths were four feet wide. The teeth were sharp blades. They could cut even a shark in half.

That's how it was for a hundred million years. For a hundred million years fishes held the center of the stage. But all the time America was getting the scenery ready for another act. America was changing. Plenty of the continent was still under water. But some of the sea was giving way to swamp. America was sea and swamp, swamp and sea, with a tract of upland here and there.

In the sea the fishes still held sway. But in the swamps a new kind of life was taking hold. Plants were coming into their own.

The climate was just as the plants liked it. The

air was warm and humid—almost tropical. It invited things to grow. In the hot-house atmosphere plants spread and uncoiled and shot up overnight.

Huge ferns bore fronds that were five and six

feet long. Scouring rushes with stalks a foot thick grew in solid stands thirty feet high. Cordaites three feet thick rose to a height of 120 feet. These were the great-great-grandparents of the pines. They were not true conifers as yet. For instead of needles they had leaves like blades.

Instead of cones, they bore long clusters of seeds.

Growing alongside these plants were other giants. Stubby-looking scale trees with a cork-like bark rose to a height of a hundred feet and more. A hundred different kinds peopled the swamps. Some were slender. Some were six feet thick. But all of them bore on the bark the scars of leaves that had dropped off, scars that looked like scales.

A vast stillness lay over the forests. The swamp muffled every sound. Neither song of bird nor hum of bee broke the silence—birds and bees had not yet come on the stage. There were huge cockroaches—four and five inches long—crawling noiselessly among the roots. In the open places dragonflies with a wing-spread of nearly thirty inches shot to and fro. But even the zoom of their great wings was deadened in the humid air.

Fern and scale tree and cordaite softly dropped their dead leaves into the black muck. Twigs and branches and tree trunks fell. The swamp accepted everything into its depths. It swallowed dead leaves, dead trees, dead seeds. It turned everything to muck. Slowly, slowly the muck became peat. Slowly, slowly the peat turned into coal. And so for hundreds of millions of years. . . .

CHAPTER 8

Reptiles Have Their Day

IT WAS FUN WATCHING THE SCIENTISTS PUT
on the great American play. They worked like
detectives solving a mystery. They would pick up
a clue here, find a trace there. And out of these
clues and traces they built the scenery and put in
the characters.

Sometimes it would happen that one set of

clues contradicted another set. Then the scientists knew they had made a mistake. They weren't stubborn. They rebuilt the scenery. Or they changed the characters to fit the facts.

There was the matter of coal, for instance. The scientists had built up the whole story out of clues they had found in the coal itself. Imprints of ferns and other leaves were there. Bits of wood, bark, leaves, roots, seed coats, lumps of resin were there. They had all turned to carbon. When scientists put the coal under a microscope, the microscope showed the same thing. No matter how formless the coal seemed, it still was the remains of plants turned to carbon. The question was: How had the plant remains got under water? For they must have done that to turn to coal.

The scientists didn't know the answer. They could only guess. So they guessed that the leaves, stems, and trunks had all been gathered up by streams and carried down into quiet pools where they had slowly turned to coal. They never thought of swamp forests. It didn't occur to the scientists that the leaves and stems and trunks had remained right where they fell. For not only did they have to imagine a forest growing in a swamp. They had to imagine that the swamp land was sinking all the time the forest was growing. Only under such conditions could thick beds of muck pile up in a swamp.

Then one day miners dug down into a layer of clay under a coal mine. There were the roots of great trees reaching down into the underclay. And there were the stumps of the trees above. Roots and stumps had turned to coal.

The scientists had to change the scenery then. It was clear that the plant remains had stayed right where they fell. A great swamp forest had once stood here. Great swamp forests must have stood in most of the places where coal beds now lay.

The scientists made other mistakes. All up and down the Connecticut Valley they had seen curious tracks in the rock. The tracks were of two large clawed feet. They were three, four, six inches, a foot and a half long.

"These must be the footprints of giant birds," the scientists thought. Then afterwards Lakes and Marsh and Cope and others had found the bones of dinosaurs in the West. Some of those dinosaurs had walked on two feet. The scientists rushed out to examine the Connecticut Valley tracks. Sure enough, they had been made by dinosaurs, not birds. The little front feet were not used to walk on; so they had left an imprint only when the dinosaur sat down.

Of course, the scientists couldn't fill in all the details. Not every plant and animal had left traces of its passing. But every year the scenery was getting surer. Every year new fossils were building up the story of life. America was a land of constant change and each age was different from the rest.

The great Coal Forests had lived their age. They were passing from the scene. For again new scenery was in the making. The earth was changing, making it harder for the swamp plants. They had to alter their ways or die. The scouring rushes shrank to tiny size. The ferns changed their habits, too. But the scale trees and cordaites were too set in their ways. All they could do was die. Evergreen forests took their place.

South of the equator it had been hot for ages.

Now suddenly it got so cold that glaciers appeared. In America the climate changed and changed again. So did the scenery. The Appalachians folded and rose into the sky. Sea bottoms came up. Dry land appeared, then went

under the sea again. Salt marshes and swamps stretched from Wyoming down to Texas.

The background was ready for the Age of Reptiles now—and they came on in countless numbers. They were little fellows at first. Later on they would be the giants whom Marsh named Terrible Lizards. But as yet there was nothing terrible about them. Many of the dinosaurs were no bigger than a cat or a crow. The biggest was not more than twelve feet long.

They made themselves at home in the uplands of New England and New Jersey. Their cousins the "false crocodiles" took over the Western salt marshes. The phytosaurs were kings of the marshes. They would lie under the shallow water by dozens and dozens with just their nostrils and eyes sticking out. They would lie and wait for prey. When they weren't hungry any more, they would waddle out on their short legs and make for the nearest sand bar. There they would drop down on their bellies among their fellows and sun themselves—and hiss—and grunt.

For millions of years the Age of Reptiles went boringly along like that. Then something happened. The scientists couldn't explain it, but for some reason or other the dinosaurs began to get bigger. They got bigger, and they got huge, and they got enormous. Dinosaurs as big as a house stomped around in the swamps. They weighed so much they could hardly stand up without water to buoy them up. Others, not very much smaller, grew frightful armor. Even the armored fishes of Age II had nothing like that to show.

The earth got so full of Terrible Lizards that some of them went into the sea. Some went up in the air. Wherever they went, there was war. It was war, war, war every day for a hundred million years. Horns and claws and teeth thrust and ripped and tore.

Then again something happened that scientists couldn't explain. Bang! the curtain came down on the Age of Reptiles. Not a single dinosaur was left.

And immediately the curtain went up again. A horde of new actors had come upon the scene. The Age of Mammals had begun.

Of course, it didn't happen by magic. The new animals didn't spring out of nothing. Already in the Age of Reptiles they had been around. But they had been just a part of the background then. What chance did a creature no bigger than a rat have beside monsters who made the earth shake when they passed? The best thing was to stay small and hide.

Now their monstrous enemies were gone. The

little mammals came out of their hiding places and took a good look around. It was a new-created world.

While the dinosaurs were making history, half of North America had been under water. A sea 500 to 1,000 miles wide had poured from the Arctic Ocean to the Gulf of Mexico. Now that sea was gone. The Rockies stood in its place. America was all dry—everywhere except just at the edges. There was plenty of room to spread and plenty of food to eat.

Wonderful seed-bearing grasses covered the ground. Wonderful trees with net-veined leaves bore fruits and nuts. Beeches and birches, maples and oaks, sweet gums and tulip trees mixed with the evergreens. Laurel, ivy, hazel-nut and holly spread over the land. A thousand flowers bloomed. A thousand insects flew and hopped and crawled and bored. Birds sang.

The little mammals took a look around at the modern world. It was exactly what they wanted. They marched out and took over America. The time was 75,000,000 years ago.

CHAPTER 9

Sabre-Tooth

THE MAMMALS WERE CERTAINLY SMALL—
but they had a number of advantages to make up
for it. They had warm blood running in their
veins. They had warm hair on their bodies. With
these they could stand cold weather a lot better
than the Terrible Lizards could.

There was another thing. Nearly all the mam-

71

mals had lost the habit of laying eggs. Instead, they gave birth to living babies. They fed those babies in a new fashion—on a curious white liquid that came out of their own bodies.

What a great freedom that meant! The creatures could keep on the go all the time. They didn't have to be tied to one place till they had finished laying a nestful of eggs. They didn't have to stay around and hatch and watch. Moreover, they could take their babies along with them from the very beginning. They could go on long journeys even across places where there was little food or none—the babies would never go hungry.

The mammals were small, but time would do a lot for them. Time would make them bigger—time always did. Time would give them better brains, better teeth, better feet. Sixty million years was a long, long time. Sixty million years would see a lot of animals coming, a lot of animals going, in America.

Just outside the city of Los Angeles lies Rancho La Brea. The ranch has a Spanish name. That's because 'way back, along with the rest of

California, it was part of Mexico. The ranch wasn't a world-famous place then. But folk did know that in that spot a black, gummy pitch came up out of the ground. When it hardened, they called it *brea*. That's Spanish for pitch.

The gummy stuff couldn't help attracting people's attention. It oozed right up out of the ground over a space that was anywhere from a mile to a quarter of a mile across. It would come up through little holes three or four inches wide. Then it would spread out into a pool. In some places it made a big pool. In some places it made a little one. Wherever it was open to the air and got mixed with the sand and dust blown into it, the pitch would harden into asphalt.

It was treacherous stuff. Around the edges the pool would be hard. A step or two farther on it would be soft. When dust covered the pool, you wouldn't know it was there; you would think it was solid earth. When it rained, the water stayed on top of the pitch. Anyone would suppose the pool was just an ordinary puddle.

Certainly plenty of beasts and birds had supposed just that. For a great many bones were mixed in with the tar. Those bones told the tale of a thousand ghastly deaths. They spoke of cattle and birds and squirrels and deer mistaking the tar for water or firm earth and being trapped in the gummy mass. They spoke of helpless animals struggling, screaming, becoming exhausted, dying.

Major Hancock, who owned Rancho La Brea, found the bones a nuisance. In the 1870's he was marketing the *brea*. It was good stuff for making pavements and was bringing him in about twenty dollars a ton. But the animal bones were a trial. The twenty-five or so Chinese who were working the *brea* had to keep getting the bones out. There were heaps of them lying around.

At the same time the Major couldn't help taking an interest in this waste material. Every once in a while some curious skull or tooth would come out of the *brea*. There was, for example, that tooth which his men had found fifteen feet down in the asphalt. The tooth was curved like a sabre. It was broken at the top, but the part that remained was all of nine and a half inches long.

The Major had never seen anything like this

tooth. It certainly didn't belong to a calf or a colt or a lamb or any other domestic creature. Nor to any wild animal he had ever seen either. What creature's could it have been?

One day Major Hancock got his chance to find out. A naturalist from Boston came out to visit the pitch pools and Major Hancock approached him.

"I should like to have your opinion, Mr. Denton," he said, "on a strange tooth I have that came out of the *brea*. Perhaps you might be able to tell me what animal has teeth like it."

They went inside.

In the back of his mind the Major had a notion that the curved tooth was going to surprise his visitor. But he wasn't at all prepared for the effect it did have on the naturalist when the tooth was laid on the table before him. Denton drew his breath in sharply. He stared at the tooth as though he couldn't believe his eyes.

"Great heavens!" he exclaimed.

For about a minute afterwards he said nothing. He just stood turning and turning the tooth over in his hand.

At last he spoke, and his voice had awe in it.

"This is the canine tooth of Machairodus," he said, "the great sabre-toothed cat that lived in the Ice Age."

Now it was Major Hancock's turn to stare. It had never occurred to him that the sabre-tooth might have belonged to a creature out of the far distant past, a creature that was no longer found on earth, a creature that was extinct. For nearly every day, it seemed to him, he was obliged to rescue a colt or a calf, a chicken or a duck, a kitten or a squirrel that had got trapped in the asphalt. Was it not natural to suppose that all the bones in the *brea* were those of cattle and other domestic animals? To think that he had been holding the tooth of a creature that had lived perhaps a hundred thousand years ago! It gave the Major the chills. He felt uncomfortable in the presence of a tooth out of the Ice Age.

"You keep it," he said to Denton.

But the naturalist hardly heard him. He had not yet come out of his dream. He stood holding the sabre-tooth in the palm of one hand and kept running the forefinger of the other over

76

the curve—inside, outside. He was thinking of what else might lie in the *brea,* of what other secrets the pitch pools held. The sabre-tooth was just a beginning, it was a key. . . .

CHAPTER 10

Death Trap of the Ages

CURIOUSLY, FOR ANOTHER THIRTY YEARS no one took the trouble to turn the key in the lock. Even the scientists forgot the sabre-tooth story Denton told.

At last one day in 1905 a geologist from Los Angeles came to look at the pitch pools. He was no great bone scholar. But he knew enough to know that not all the bones belonged to modern animals. He got together some samples, showed them to a friend, then took the friend down to Rancho La Brea.

The friend was impressed. "This place is nothing less than a Death Trap of the Ages," he said. "There's no telling what may be in that asphalt."

He dug around and picked out a few skulls and bones. "I'm going to take these to John Merriam at the University of California," he said. "Merriam is tops in this sort of thing. Right now he is investigating the very creatures whose bones these were. This package is going to make a sensation."

He was more than right. Professor Merriam no sooner heard where the bones came from than he prepared to dash down to Rancho La Brea. He felt like a man who has been left an unexpected fortune.

Yet when he got down to the pools and started to dig, John Merriam saw that the treasure was far greater than he could ever have imagined. All the bone collections in all the museums of the world held nothing to compare with it for this period of time.

The asphalt of Rancho La Brea housed a huge menagerie of the Ice Age. Sabre-tooth tigers with monstrous claws were there by the dozens. Lions bigger than their African descendants were there. Great wolves by the hundreds, vultures, imperial elephants, mammoths, mastodons, giant ground sloths as big as oxen were there. Horses and camels and llamas of a hundred thousand years ago mingled their bones with those of familiar barnyard creatures. Animals that the American scientists had never heard about were there. Animals that seemed to belong to Africa rather than America were there as well.

John Merriam worked and brought others to work with him. There was so much to do! The bones were so thick in the asphalt that it was impossible to get out some without hurting others. In places they formed a tangled, matted mass. But bit by bit the strange menagerie was stepping out of the *brea*. Bit by bit the Ice Age was coming to life.

The scientists could not help noting how strange this menagerie was. Not only were the animals different from any living creature in

America or anywhere else. The whole character of the menagerie was different.

Merriam and the others knew that in any collection of bones there were always more bones of herb-eating animals than of flesh-eating ones. It had to be that way. That's the way animal life was. If there were too many flesh-eaters, they would soon finish off all the herb-eaters and have nothing left to feed upon. Then they would have to eat one another till all were gone. But in this menagerie there were more flesh-eaters than there were all other kinds of animals put together.

Why was that?

Another peculiar thing was that nearly all the animals were either very old or very young. If they were neither of these, then they were certain to be diseased or maimed. Many a sabre-tooth tiger had a sabre broken off. Many of the wolves and other creatures had limbs that had broken and healed.

Why was that?

John Merriam had plenty of time to think about these things while he worked. Also he had plenty of opportunity to observe. He watched with the greatest curiosity to see what ranch creatures would get trapped in the pools. "The present," he said to himself, "is a guide to the past. What happens here today must be the very thing that happened over and over again a hundred thousand years ago."

So he watched. He watched and could not help noticing that always it was a young and inexperienced creature that got trapped. Horses and cows knew enough to keep away. It was the colts and calves who got into trouble.

Merriam heard the same thing from others. In Ventura County, where there were pitch pools like those of Rancho La Brea, colts were always getting trapped. It was necessary on a certain ranch, when the summer sun had melted the tar, to have someone ride the range every day to pull out the colts who had got stuck.

Yes, it was easy enough for a young, inexperienced creature to get into trouble. The boundary between hard asphalt and soft tar was very vague. Merriam himself often could not tell where it was safe to step. His eyes were of no use to him. Only by actually trying the tar with his feet could he tell where the hard outer ring of the pools ended and where the dangerous soft part began. Young, inexperienced creatures did not test the tar cautiously. They went unsuspectingly forward until it was too late. And once in, only a creature in the prime of strength could free itself.

How many times towards the end of the day Merriam would see the same act repeated! In the dim light the pitchy lake would look very much like water. Birds would come down and settle on it as if on water. Little mice would run out too fast. Both would find themselves caught, bound, unable to pull themselves out. Then from the surrounding trees owls would fly down to feed on the mice and the birds. And in their turn they, too, would get caught in the gummy mass.

To Merriam it was a living example of what had been. When for the first time he saw the owls coming down to feed on the entangled birds and mice, the answer to the riddle of the pools suddenly came to him. He understood why there were so many more flesh-eaters than other creatures in the menagerie. The tar pools were more than just a trap. They were a trap that was forever being baited anew with fresh meat.

As in a vision John Merriam saw the cruel play that had been enacted time and again upon this spot. . . .

Out of the forest glade he saw a ground sloth come lumbering along on clumsy feet. It is the day's end. The creature is not stopping now to dig up plants with his enormous digging claws. He is thirsty. He is looking for a water hole, and from a distance he thinks he sees one. It is the deceiving gleam of the tar pool which he takes for water. He breaks into a trot, blunders into the pool. Then he stops short, surprised.

Angrily he pulls one gummy foot out and shakes it. He does not know that already it is too late to retreat—the other feet are sinking deeper into the tar. He struggles, struggles desperately to get free. He cannot pull himself out—there is nothing to push against, no bottom that his feet can touch. He is trapped. He cannot get back. A loud, despairing cry comes from his throat.

Far and near that terrible cry rings. Herb-eating animals raise their heads and shudder and hide themselves when they hear it. But the sabre-tooth tigers rejoice. The wolves rejoice.

The vultures rejoice. All the flesh-eating creatures hearing that cry move in the direction
from which it comes.

The sabre-tooths stand on the edge of the pool.
They watch the floundering, helpless sloth with
hungry eyes. Then with a snarl one of them leaps
on the creature's back, digs in his monstrous
claws and with his great sabres stabs at the neck
again and again. The sloth stops floundering.
His terrible cry no longer fills the air.

Now a second sabre-tooth and a third take the
fatal leap. The three snarl and fight to possess the
prey. They are so busy they do not at first real-
ize that they, too, are caught in the gummy mass.
One, the strongest, pulls away. He clambers out
over the backs of the others, leaps to safety.

On the edge of the pool wolves stand hungrily
watching. In their turn they, too, spring into
the baited trap—to meet the same terrible end.
Now from the trees round about there comes a
flapping of great wings. Vultures are coming
down to feed on sloth and sabre-tooth and wolf.
The cruel beaks tear into the living flesh. But as
they do so, the flapping wings dip into the tar.
The vultures, too, are imprisoned. . . .

How many times had this same play been repeated?

John Merriam wouldn't even guess. He thought of the seventeen sabre-tooth and wolf skulls that had come out of a single cubic yard of asphalt.

"Over and over again," was all he could say.

CHAPTER 11

Up on One Toe

Back in the days when marsh was discovering flying dragons and birds with teeth, he
gave America yet another surprise. He dug up
the fossil remains of a horse.

"What?" people snapped at him. "Horses in
America? Everybody knows there were no
horses in America till the white men came.

Everybody knows that when the Indians saw Spaniards on horseback they were scared to death. Don't you remember? They thought horse and rider were one animal."

But it was a horse. Not a very big one but still a horse. You could tell by the teeth. You could tell by the feet.

After that a lot of people scurried around looking for horses. For scientists—and other people, too—were curious about the horse's family tree. Of all animals the horse is the most intelligent. Of all animals the horse has done the most for man. People wanted to know its story. Where had the horse come from? Who were its ancestors? How did it spread through the world? Did it really die out in America? And if so, why?

So a lot of people dug for horses. For the most part this digging was just haphazard. One man would have a hunch and dig here. Another would have a hunch and dig there. Sometimes a person would be digging for something entirely different and just happen to find a horse. But there were museum expeditions, too. One of these went on for three years and covered nearly all the West. From the plains of Texas, through

New Mexico, through eastern Colorado, through western Nebraska, and up into Montana the exploring parties went searching for horses.

Altogether, with this and that, hundreds of skeletons came out of the rocks. And out of the hundreds of skeletons came a story. It was more wonderful than that of any other animal. It was a story of streamlining for speed. It was a story of keeping pace with changing America. It was a story of success through better brains, better feet, better teeth.

The story opens 50,000,000 years ago. The mammals have only recently taken the country over. It is the morning of the Modern World. The Mississippi flows lazily into the Gulf of Mexico, but the river's mouth is up at Cairo, Illinois. The Rockies are in place, but they are not high and bold as when the last of the dinosaurs ruled the land. Time has planed them down. They will not be high again for another many million years.

All over America it is warm. There are palms and alligators in the Dakotas—you would think it was Florida. Up in Alaska giant redwoods are growing along with beeches and chestnuts and elms. Even magnolias and fig trees prosper there.

Gone are the great marshes of the West. It is a land of lakes and forests now. But there are park-like openings in the forest where soft green grass is growing. And that's where we see him first, the little hero of our story—Eohippus, the Dawn Horse. He is with his herd. They are cropping the soft green grass.

The little creatures are really tiny—they are no bigger than foxes. They stand just eleven inches high at the shoulder. They are graceful little animals with arched backs and flowing tails. On their front feet they have four toes. On the hind feet they have only three.

You would never think that the future belongs to these little creatures. They are so delicate, so shy, so nervous. They are ready to start and run at the slightest sound. For they have enemies. The foxes love to hunt them. So they run, run, trying to outrun the foxes. Their safety lies in their little hoofed feet. If they can't outrun the foxes, they are lost.

It is a race in which size would help—longer legs can take a longer stride. So over millions of years Nature weeds out the smallest, Nature weeds out the weakest. The little Dawn Horse grows. He gets to be big as a collie dog.

He lives more and more out in the open now. For while he was growing America changed again. The West is great tracts of prairie land with slow rivers winding through and trees growing just along the water courses. The prairies are covered with grass. It is still the same soft green grass. The little horses can chew it with their simple teeth. But even so the teeth don't last long. Ten or twelve years and the little horse, for all his running, must die because his teeth are worn out.

Something has to be done about that. The teeth have got to get higher so they'll last longer. Something has to be done about the feet, too. Already one of the toes has disappeared. There are only three toes on each of the little feet, but all of them still rest on the ground in walking. The way to get speed is to rise up on your toes. Even little Eohippus did that. If you can get up on one toe, you will be faster still. Already there are signs that this is going to happen. Though all the toes still touch the ground, the middle toe is distinctly larger than the others.

Not all the little horses have the same problems to solve. For the plains are not the only places where horses live. There are little forest horses, too. The ground they walk on is soft. So nothing needs to be done about their toes and they stay long and lie flat on the ground. The teeth don't change either. There is no need to change when you feed on leaves and browse instead of grazing. So there is much less wear on their teeth.

But the horses of the plains must definitely change if they are going to survive. For the grass is changing. It is no longer the soft green grass it used to be. It is harsh and dry. It wears the teeth down faster. The teeth have got to get longer. Some way, too, has to be found to make the surface of the teeth uneven so they can grind the tough grass better.

And size and speed have got to increase. For now it is no longer foxes that are the enemy. It is wolves and giant dogs. Speed, speed to get away! Strength, strength to kick hard!

The little horses get to be as big as Shetland ponies. The limbs are long for running. The side toes get off the ground. The little horse creature is up on one toe now. Like a ballet dancer, he scarcely seems to touch the ground.

After that it is just a question of time—the little plains horse is well on the way to being an almost perfect mechanism. The dangling, useless side toes will soon go. For Nature will keep nothing that is useless.

The short-lived teeth will go, too. Already they keep on growing for a longer period of time. But there is something else in the making. A new and brilliant scheme is being tried. The thin enamel is being surrounded by cement to keep the teeth from breaking. Inside, the soft dentine wears down faster than the enamel. So the enamel stands up in ridges. There is always a jagged grinding surface that is just right for the tough prairie grass.

A few more million years and there he stands —Equus, the modern horse, he who is to be the friend and servant of man.

It has taken 40,000,000 years to make him. It has taken countless experiments to make him. But he is worth it. He is swift and intelligent, beautiful, strong. He is more perfect than any other mammal. He can outrun the swiftest of his enemies. He can travel great distances at a stretch. He is powerful; he can ward off anything with his hoofs. He is invisible; his color is so like his surroundings you can scarcely see him cropping the grass. He can endure the cold; his hairy coat thickens to protect him. He doesn't

ask much in the way of food. The rough dry grass is food enough for him—his wonderful teeth can take care of it. They are made to wear. They can stand twenty-five and thirty years of constant grinding.

There he stands, ready for man's taming hand. But it will be a long time yet. Man will be his enemy before he is his friend. There will be thousands of years of hunting the horse before man thinks of driving him. There will be thousands of years more before man thinks of riding him. It will be a long, long story yet.

And none of it will happen in America. In America the horse will not wait to see the coming of man.

What? Not wait? After 40,000,000 years in America? After countless times of trying this and trying that? After proudly trekking on one toe up and down the two Americas and out over the land bridges into Asia and Europe?

The scientists shrugged their shoulders. It wasn't their fault if the story the skeletons told seemed unreasonable. To all appearance the horse had vanished. Before the Indians came, it had disappeared. That's all they knew about it. It had been hard enough for the scientists to believe it themselves. But hadn't they dug and dug for horses in all the places where forgotten Indians had lived long ago? They hadn't found the bones of a single horse. The horse had simply disappeared.

How could they explain it?

Had the cold of the Ice Age killed him off? But in Europe the horse had lived right through the Ice Age—there were his pictures scratched and painted on the cave man's walls.

Was it disease? Had an epidemic wiped him out in America?

Perhaps. But could anyone know for sure?

The one thing certain was that he had lived, and experimented, and died in America. The one thing sure was that he had come back a stranger to his native land.

CHAPTER 12

Boiling Hot, Ice Cold

ALL THE WHILE THAT NATURE WAS EXPERI-
menting with horses, America kept changing
and changing. Rain and snow and frost and wind
were doing their work. They ate away at the
mountains. They bit off chunks, they carried off
grains.

97

Down, down, down. The Rockies got lower and lower. The basins between the mountains got filled to the brim with stuff from the mountains. By the time *Moropus* and the rhinos and the giant pig came wandering along the Niobrara, almost nothing of the Rockies showed. Only here and there, especially hard chunks of mountain—Monadnocks—remained. They were all that was left to mark the places where the ranges had been.

Then again the earth began to labor. Again the region was lifted up. Again rain and frost and snow and wind began to carve the mountains. Old rivers that had been flowing along lazily grew young again as they rushed and leaped down newly cut mountainsides. Down, down, down. Down through the plateaus they cut, down across the filled-in basins, down across the mountain ranges lying buried in their own waste. Gorges and canyons appeared.

All over the West the crust of the earth was restless. A great change was taking place. The Sierra Nevadas were thrust up, the Cascade Mountains rose. And deep down under the earth there was a seething and a boiling such as had not occurred since the crust of the earth first formed.

Over great areas of the West new crust was being made. Boiling hot rock came pouring out of the earth. The lava welled up through cracks in the weak part of the crust. It spread out like a sea. In western Washington and Oregon and Idaho it covered an area bigger than all New England. In Colorado it built up the plateau where Yellowstone Park would stand.

Every few hundred years a great flow of boiling hot rock would spread over the region and kill every living thing upon it. It would bury great forests. Years would pass, tens and hundreds of years would pass. The buried trees would turn to stone. New forests would start growing on top. And again molten rock would well up and bury them. Over and over again it would happen. In the Yellowstone it happened eighteen times. Eighteen layers of stone forest remained to tell the tale of what had been.

In other parts of the West the earth's crust burst open violently. Volcanoes shot clouds of steam and dust high into the air. In central Oregon they spouted so much volcanic ash that the John Day Basin got filled with it half a mile deep. All over the West thousands of volcanoes spouted lava and cinders. All over the West the lava and cinders piled up into cones. Some of the cones were not more than twenty to 600 feet high. Mount Hood and Mount Rainier and Mt. Shasta towered among them, smoking, spouting, exploding.

Then peace again. Down underneath, the lava still seethed. The geysers of boiling water in Colorado showed that. Deep down underneath the earth's crust the lava was still hot enough to turn water into steam and shoot it sky high. But the lava no longer came pouring out. America had nearly finished her adventure with heat. She was starting a new adventure—this time with cold.

Already a long time back the climate had begun to change. It was getting moister. In Utah the streams from the mountains started pouring so much water into the great basin that it turned into a lake. Lake Bonneville filled a thousand feet deep. It covered 20,000 square miles. The mountains of Utah looked like hilly islands in the midst of a fresh-water sea.

It was getting colder, too. You couldn't notice it from year to year. You couldn't notice it from century to century. But up in Alaska magnolias and figs weren't comfortable any more. Palms and alligators didn't do so well in the Dakotas.

Gone were the days of easy living—now it was move or perish.

Up on the mountains the snow lay around later into the spring. Then it didn't go away at all. It piled up in thicker and thicker drifts, it turned to ice underneath, it started to move. All over the northern hemisphere it was the same. Glaciers were forming, ice sheets were forming.

In America they pushed out from two great centers. The center of one was in Labrador; the center of the second was by Hudson Bay. A third great ice sheet formed over western Canada.

The ice sheets pushed out north and south and east and west. They spread and spread till all of Canada was under a single ice cap. A mile thick, two miles thick the ice cap grew at the centers. So much water went into the making of the ice that the level of the oceans went down. The drowned edges of America came up. You could walk over dry land from Alaska to Asia. So thick was the ice that Canada could not bear the weight and sagged beneath it.

Nothing could stop the ice. It moved north up to the Pole. It moved south over the White Mountains, south over the Adirondacks, south over the Rockies. It gouged and scoured and ground and polished. It carved the mountains. It turned V-shaped valleys into U's. It stripped the soil from monster tracts of Canada and bore it along. It plucked a million boulders and took them with it. It scooped a thousand hollows in Canada's bare bedrock. It gouged out the Great Lakes basins. It changed the face of everything it passed over.

Just creeping. Just a few feet a year. But never stopping. Sixteen hundred miles from its centers the glacier traveled.

The pall of death lay over the icy wastes of America. But down below the ice belt a wonderful life was astir. Down below the ice belt America was a big game country.

Four different kinds of elephants roamed the land. In the Southern Great Plains imperial elephants, fourteen feet high at the shoulder, carried around tusks thirteen feet long. In the desert basins of Arizona and Nevada slightly smaller elephants ranged. Herds of mastodons browsed in the forests of the East.

And in front of the glacier and right on the ice itself woolly mammoths tramped around. What cared they for ice and snow! Snug under their brown wool, they thought nothing of going right up to the Arctic, from which even the musk-ox and the reindeer had fled.

Buffaloes in vast herds roamed the Great Plains of the South. Hundreds of thousands of years later white men would find just such great herds in the Central Plains. But they would never see seven different kinds of buffaloes. They would not see huge beasts with a hornspread of six feet.

Nor would they see ten kinds of horses, camels of all sorts, wild pigs, sabre-tooth tigers, huge lumbering ground sloths, armadillos, glyptodonts.

All these swarmed in America. They turned the land into a great zoo. Yet all the time, a few miles off, the glacier was busy spreading death. Tongues of ice pushed here, pushed there.

Then suddenly the ice cap started to melt.

Icy streams poured from the melting front of the glacier. New rivers sprang up. Splendid waterfalls appeared. The stolen soil of Canada dropped, burying the valleys of the north central States. Drift and boulders spread over New England. The Great Lakes basins filled with icy water. To the west of them shallow Lake Agassiz, five times bigger than Lake Superior, formed. As long as the ice stayed, the monster lake would stand there. Its bottom would make the fertile wheat land of North Dakota and the Red River Valley of Manitoba.

But not yet. Not for thousands of years yet. The ice had come and the ice was going—but it would come again. Three times more it would come down again, gouging, scraping, scouring. It would reshape America. It would leave behind a new-created world.

CHAPTER 13

The Great Debate

BUT WHERE ALL THIS TIME WAS MAN? ALONG with the four kinds of elephants, the seven kinds of bison, and the ten kinds of horses, was there not any kind of man?

This was the question Americans were asking. They knew that in other parts of the world the bones of man different from our own kind had been found. In Java, in England, in China, in Africa, men who were not of the *Homo sapiens* variety like us had existed long ago. Some had lived as long as a quarter of a million years ago. Some had lived as long as a million years ago.

Much later Neanderthal man had left his bones and his tools and weapons in European caves. That had been anywhere from a hundred thousand to thirty thousand years ago. And after him had come other men of the Ice Age. They, too, had been great hunters. On the walls of the caves they lived in they had painted pictures of the Ice Age beasts they hunted—woolly mammoths and reindeer, bison, wild boars, horses.

Yes, everybody knew that twenty-five thousand years ago our caveman ancestors had lived in France and Spain. But what about cave men in America? Were the Indians the first people of the New World? Or had there been other kinds of men there before them?

People asked these questions. But the scientists couldn't answer. They talked about it, of course. Some said it wasn't possible for man to have sprung up in America. They said there were no apes from which man could have developed. Others said we hadn't looked long enough. They said that if we searched hard, we would find dawn-men just as we had found dawn-horses.

Every once in a while there was a flurry of excitement. The newspapers would announce that somebody had dug up a mysterious skeleton. They said it was terribly old. Scientists would rush to the spot to look at the bones. And like as not they would find that somebody was playing them a trick.

Once Othniel Marsh went to take a look at such a skeleton. A good many other people did, too. The men who dug it up were getting rich charging folk for the privilege of looking at it. People said the bones were so old they had turned to stone. Well, the skeleton was stone, all right. But it was no fossil. The owners of the "Cardiff Giant" had buried him first and dug him up afterwards. The skeleton had been carved out of gypsum!

Once, though, the scientists thought they

really had something. Harold Cook, the son of that James Cook on whose ranch the rhinos had been found, discovered a worn old tooth which set everybody talking.

Scientists agreed that the "Nebraska tooth" was definitely human. It was very ancient, they said. They said it was older even than the Java man, and he had lived maybe half a million years ago. They photographed the cracked old tooth. They radiographed it. They compared it with ancient ape teeth and with every human tooth that had ever been found.

"It is strangely like and unlike the other teeth," the scientists said.

Some said the "Nebraska tooth" proved definitely that dawn-men had sprung up in America. Others said the dawn-men had not sprung up in America but had wandered in from Siberia along with the animals.

The tooth made news for some time—and then suddenly the scientists changed their minds. It was all a mistake, they said. The "Nebraska tooth" had belonged to an ancient pig.

No matter how many times they were disappointed, some of the scientists still kept hoping. And every little while something would be found to lift their spirits high. Human bones would be dug up lying alongside mammoth and mastodon bones.

"There!" some scientists would say. "Doesn't that prove that man lived in America during the Ice Age?"

"Not at all," others would say. "All it proves is that the mammoth and the mastodon lived much closer to our own times than we suppose. These human skulls are too much like our own to be as old as you say. Skulls from the Ice Age would be very different."

A great deal was said, a great deal of ink flowed—but it was nothing to what went on when the "Minnesota Man" was found.

That happened in 1931.

In that year some workmen were digging a road in what had once been the bottom of an Ice Age lake. Ten feet down they came upon a human skeleton. Was this a grave, they wondered? Had somebody been buried here? It didn't look like a burial. It looked as if the soil had never been disturbed. It looked as if the

earth had been collecting naturally on top of the bones for thousands of years until it was ten feet thick.

Professor Jenks of the University of Minnesota rushed hotfoot out to see the bones. It was a wonderful chance. This find might hold the answer to the question everybody was asking. It might reveal for how many thousands of years man had lived in America.

But disappointment was waiting for him. Before Professor Jenks arrived, the workmen had taken the bones from their resting place. The professor's chance to see the skeleton in place was gone.

He could hardly choke down his disappointment. Not that he didn't believe the men. He did. But he knew that other people would not take their word for it. If he, on the other hand, a scientist, said the skeleton had been found ten feet down under undisturbed soil, his word would most likely have been accepted. Now it was all spoiled.

He took a quick look at the bones, then got down into the pit. And then the lucky thing happened. Not all of the skeleton had been removed! Two little bits of bone had been overlooked. The bits fitted exactly into the other bones. So he had proof positive after all. After all he could say that the skeleton had really come from ten feet down under the lake bottom! It would be too unlikely that the workmen had thrown the bits of bone back into the pit in order to deceive the public.

In great excitement he returned to search the pit again. And again luck was with the professor. Two curious objects now came to his hand. One was a knife made out of elk horn. It had a little hole at one end. The other was a conch shell. It had two little holes in it. Both objects, he decided, must have been worn by the person whose skeleton this was. Perhaps the shell had hung from a thong around the neck. Perhaps the knife had been suspended from a girdle.

As for the skeleton itself, the professor saw immediately that it wasn't a man's at all. The papers all had headlines about the "Minnesota Man." He must set them straight—the "Minnesota Man" was really a girl about fifteen years old. Twenty thousand years ago she had drowned in this glacial lake.

Professor Jenks was satisfied that the problem was solved now. He had no idea that he had only started another argument.

"If the skull is as old as you say," one very learned scientist said, "it ought to be quite different from modern man's."

"It is," Professor Jenks replied. "The jaws stick out very far and the teeth are extraordinarily large. They are bigger even than those of some of the cave men of Europe."

"But this is a *Homo sapiens* skull!" insisted the other scientist.

"I agree with you. It is a *Homo sapiens* skull," Jenks answered. "But it is a *very early type*."

The other authority said: "The skeleton was all together when found. If this girl drowned, her bones would have been scattered by the water."

"Not necessarily," Professor Jenks replied. "Not if the water was very cold. In cold water the skeleton would have fallen apart very slowly. Sand would have had a chance to cover and keep the bones together."

The very learned scientist remained unconvinced. "It is my opinion," he said baldly, "that this Minnesota girl was a Sioux Indian. In my study of Sioux skulls I have seen every one of the things you point out as being different."

"But you have never seen *all* of these different things in any *one* skull!" Jenks retorted.

And so it went—on and on. Nearly everybody took sides. Some people believed the skull was 20,000 years old and some said it belonged to a Sioux Indian.

But a few people weren't quite ready to make up their minds. "Let's wait for more evidence," they said.

CHAPTER 14

Bison Hunt

EVIDENCE THAT MAN HAD LIVED IN AMER-
ica a very long time had all the while been pil-
ing up. It was not the evidence of bones. It was
the evidence of stones.

It all started five years before the "Minnesota
Man" was found.

In the year 1926 a group of scientists from

115

the Colorado Museum of Natural History were digging for fossil bones near the little town of Folsom, New Mexico. They were having a good season. Deep down under clay and gravel they were finding quantities of just what they were looking for. They were digging up the remains of a kind of bison that everybody believed had died out long ago.

Now it is very exciting to find what you are looking for. But it is much more exciting to find what you are not looking for. And this is just what happened. Out of the loose dirt the diggers had thrown up with their shovels, one of the scientists picked out two pieces of chipped flint. The chipping, he saw at once, could never have been done by Nature. It had been done by man. Man had been here. These chipped bits of stone had been his weapons. The question was: How long ago had he lived? Had he been here at the same time as the bison?

The scientist had not found the chipped flints in place. The little pieces had been flung up along with the dirt. To prove that man and the bison had been on this spot together the scientists had to find a chipped stone lying right on the same level as the bison bones. Now one of the flints was broken. Could they by any chance find the other half?

Hoping against hope, they left the loose dirt and returned to the pit. They had put by their spades. Such rough digging wouldn't serve them now. From now on they would pare the earth away with knives. They would scrape it away by thimblefuls. Only so could they be sure of leaving any chip they found in place.

Their eyes were riveted on the ground. Each man was silently praying for a little bit of luck.

And then it happened. Imbedded in the clay around a rib bone of one of the bison lay a little piece of chipped flint. The scientists didn't know yet if this was the bit of stone they had hoped to find. They didn't dare take it out to see. They knew they had to preserve the flint right in place so they could prove to anyone who doubted it that bone and flint had been found side by side. So they carefully cut out the whole block of clay and sent it to the museum laboratory.

There was a big to-do then. Scientists came from here and scientists came from there. Pictures were taken. There was an ocean of talk.

And finally the flint was taken out of the clay. Then it became clear that this was the very bit they had been looking for. It fitted exactly into the broken piece they had found in the loose dirt. Together the two bits made a point for a dart.

Surely everyone would be convinced now!

But not at all. Nearly all the scientists in America refused to believe it. They wouldn't listen to the theory that the chipped flint had been hurled at the bison by means of a dart thrower. It was impossible, they said. This kind of bison, they said, had died out in the Ice Age. And there were no men in America then.

"But how did the chipped flint get there?" the Colorado Museum people demanded.

The scientists said they didn't know. It had somehow worked its way in, they said.

J. D. Figgins, the Director of the Museum, could hardly restrain himself. It was ridiculous to carry doubt so far. The proof was clear, he said. There was the bison's rib bone. There was the dart point. Anybody could read the story—a dart had stuck in the bison's side. The flesh had rotted away, the stone had remained. People wanted more proof? All right, he would get it.

When the next season started, Figgins ordered the digging to begin on the very same spot. He felt certain he was only at the beginning of the story. Why were there so many bison bones here? Was it not because this was the scene of a great hunt of long ago? And if it was so, weren't the diggers bound to find many more dart points here?

His guess was right. The digging had been going on only a short time when four more broken points showed up. Unfortunately, carefully as they worked, the scientists were not careful enough; every one of the points was loosened from the clay before its exact position could be marked. But at last a fifth point appeared. And it was stuck firmly in the clay on the very same level as the bison bones!

There was his evidence. Figgins immediately ordered the work to stop. Telegrams were sent right and left to all the leading institutions. "Come and see for yourselves."

Three great authorities from three great institutions hurried to the spot. And this time they agreed. They couldn't help believing in spite of themselves. Everything pointed to Folsom, New Mexico as the scene of a great hunt. In the first place, all the dart points were broken. That could mean only one thing: The hunters had done just what Indian hunters do today—they had retrieved and carried away the unbroken points to use again. Also, there were almost no tails among the bison remains. And what could that mean except that the animals had been skinned? The tails had gone along with the hides.

Still the question remained: When? When did the hunt take place? Ten to twenty thousand years ago? Or much more recently? Did the Folsom bison die out in the Ice Age? Or did they live through the bad times and die out much nearer to our own time?

It was anybody's guess. The evidence was there, but no one could say exactly what it meant.

CHAPTER 15

Secret of Gypsum Cave

Meantime more facts were gathering.
Other scientists were digging in other places.
They were finding that the extinct bison was not
the only animal of long ago that man had hunted.
Many a mammoth and mastodon had been felled
by the darts of ancient Americans. In fact, it began to look as if the first discoverers of America

had got acquainted with a whole host of animals that were now extinct.

There was the evidence from Gypsum Cave, for example.

Gypsum Cave is a limestone cavern in Nevada. It lies sixteen miles from Las Vegas and is a big cavern with five connecting chambers. Until 1924 it had been left strictly alone. But in that year Mark Harrington of the Southwest Museum visited it. He had immediately fallen under its spell. For there was something different about this cavern, something he had never met before. There was a secret here. What was it?

Even that very first time, Harrington had seen that the cavern had been inhabited by man. Right at the entrance he had found broken bits of pottery. He had recognized them as belonging to Pueblo Indians. But somehow from the first he felt sure that the Pueblos were not the earliest inhabitants of Gypsum Cave. People older than the Pueblos had lived here, and before them—who knew?—perhaps even animals that were now extinct.

As soon as Harrington began to poke about the cave floor he saw that his guess was right. A people older than the Pueblos had indeed lived here, for they had left behind long wooden darts with stone tips. Such darts, he knew, had been used in America about 2,000 years ago. But the curious thing was that these ancient darts lay right on the surface of the floor. Things 2,000 years old don't generally lie on the surface but deep down under the soil. If things 2,000 years old lay right on the surface, how old would things under the floor be?

He began to dig test holes here and there in the cavern floor. Now what was his surprise to find that the 2,000-year-old darts rested on manure. It was dung different from any Harrington had ever seen before. It must be, he supposed, the dung of an animal that was now extinct. What animal could it be?

He examined the manure closely. It was very full of thready material—the animal must have been a vegetarian, then.

"Now what kind of extinct plant-eating animal could crawl into a hole like this cave?" Harrington asked himself.

Only the giant ground sloth, he decided. But the giant ground sloth was supposed to have died out in the Ice Age. Supposing he were to find that man had been here at the same time as the ground sloth! What would the scientists say about that?

In 1930 Harrington was back in the cave with several assistants. And now his guess was to be proved right. Hidden behind a slab of rock lay a complete ground sloth's skull. Down in the dirt of the floor lay his huge horny claws. His shaggy reddish hair was there and even bits of his hide.

But what about man? Had man come to Gypsum Cave after the sloth had died? Or had he hunted the animal? This was the question the excited diggers wanted answered.

They didn't have long to wait. They had now cut down through the manure. Now they could see what lay underneath, and it was something quite unbelievable. They were finding dart shafts. Human beings had lived in Gypsum Cave even *before* the ground sloths had occupied it!

Harrington and his assistants exchanged glances. What would the scientists say about their discovery? They probably wouldn't believe that man had occupied the cave before the ground sloths lived there. They would probably say it was impossible. They would say the dart shafts had somehow slipped through the manure.

Well, let them doubt. Harrington and his assistants *knew*. And the best evidence of all was the campfire some of the party had found near the cavern entrance. They had dug down through seven feet of broken rock, stalagmites, and sloth dung. Under everything they had found the ashes. Surely the ashes hadn't "somehow slipped through."

No, there was no question about it. Man and the ground sloth had lived in the cave turn and turn about. But when had this been?

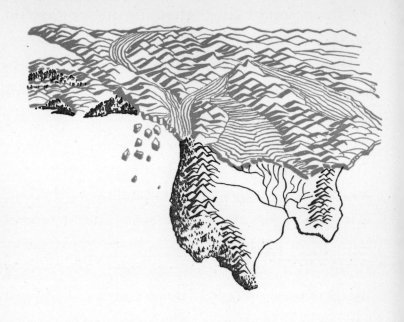

CHAPTER 16

The First Americans

I T WAS ALL VERY CONFUSING. THE EVIDENCE was so strong. It looked so positive that man had lived in America along with the extinct bison and mammoth and mastodon and giant ground sloth. But did that mean there were men in America in the Ice Age?

126

No one could say. Perhaps no one ever would be able to say.

That didn't prevent people from having opinions, though. They kept right on arguing about it. They would bring up all sorts of proof. They would say:

"Look at maize. Maize is the most helpless of all grains. It has lost the power to take care of itself. Never, never does anybody find a stalk of corn growing by itself. Think for how many thousands of years maize must have been tended by the Indians to get as helpless as that. At least 10,000."

Or they would say: "Think of the Indian languages. In the time of Columbus in the region north of Mexico the Indians spoke 500 different languages. In California alone they spoke well over a hundred. One group couldn't understand another. Yet the Eskimos of Siberia and Alaska and Greenland, though they don't see each other very often, still understand one another's speech. Think how long it must have taken for the Indian languages to become so different!"

But one thing the scientists were pretty well

agreed on. Nearly all of them had come to believe that there had been no dawn-men in America. At some unknown date in the past Indians had discovered America.

But where had the Indians come from?

That was something people had all sorts of ideas about.

Some said: "The Indians came from the lost Continent of Atlantis which once lay where the Atlantic flows today."

Some said: "The Indians came from the Lost Continent of Mu which once lay where the Pacific flows today."

Some said: "They came from the South Sea Islands."

Some said: "From China."

Some said: "From Egypt."

"The Indians," others claimed, "are the lost tribes of Israel."

"They are descendants of the Welsh."

"They are descended from the Vikings."

People argued and argued. But little by little, as they learned more and more, most of the scientists came to agree about it. "The one possible place the great mass of Indians could have come from," they said, "is Asia. They came across Bering Strait. At that point only fifty-six miles divide Asia from America. Moreover, the distance is broken by three islands. Even on cloudy days you can look across and see land. Besides, in ancient days there may have been a land bridge all the way."

It seemed unbelievable that all the many millions of settlers had come that way. Yet nearly everybody agreed. The scholars looked across Bering Strait and down across thousands of years and on the other shore they saw the first discoverers of America standing.

They were a straggly little group—an old man or two, a few young men, some women, children, dogs. They looked ill-fed. They looked travel-worn. They had wandered so long, so far. They had found so little. They peered across Bering Strait with eyes dimmed by campfire smoke and ice glare. Perhaps in that other land life would be easier, the hunting better. . . .

And so the crossing was made. From the Old World, for which they had no name—to the New, for which they had no name either. For the first time now, but over and over again in the thousands of years to come. By just such little groups, each knowing nothing of the others, America would be discovered again and again.

Down across the frozen tundra; down through the cone-bearing forests; around the rivers; over the mountains; following the caribou, the straggly groups of Indians came. A few here, a few there, always increasing, always moving, spreading, discovering.

The Indians gave names to the lakes, to the rivers, the mountains, the trees, the strange new beasts. Whatever the thing looked like to them, by that name they called it. Sometimes the name stuck. Sometimes other groups of wanderers, coming after, called it by the same name.

Down in the Southern Plains they met the bison. That was the most important thing that happened to them. The bison was a beast made to fit all the Indians' needs. Gone now were the days of hunger. Gone were the days of cold. Here was plentiful meat, here was durable hide, long warm hair, bone, horn. The Indians followed the bison.

Why did any of them go farther? Why didn't

they stay where food was plentiful, where the climate was good?

Who knows all the thinking of man?

Some of the Indians moved on. Into the tropical-rain forest; across mountain-hung valleys; over grassy plains; down to the cold, dreary land's end. Indians stood on Tierra del Fuego at the tip of South America and looked off into the Polar Sea. Indians stood in Alaska and looked off into the Arctic.

All the New World was their home. But they had no name for it. Each group knew only the place where it had come to rest. Each knew nothing of the others. Each called itself "The People," or "The real People," or "Our Own Folk." No man remembered where his ancestors had come from. No man knew how far his ancestors had trekked. Can any man remember back over thousands of years?

They didn't know much, these discoverers, going from the unremembered land into the unknown. They came bringing just two skills with them. They knew how to hunt, and they knew how to chip stone into weapons and tools. But they were ready for learning. They knew how to adapt themselves to desert and jungle, to forest and plain, to mountain and sea shore, to heat and cold, to drought and rain.

CHAPTER 17

The Wetherill Boys Go Exploring

Down in the southwest corner of Colorado in the 1890's there lived a family named Wetherill. They were Quaker ranchers. All summer long the boys of the family worked hard tending cattle. But in the fall and winter they would go out to seek adventures. For this was old Indian country. Sometimes the boys would come home bringing a bit of pottery they had dug up. Sometimes they would bring tales of caves and skeletons and ruined dwellings they had seen.

One winter the eldest of the boys—Richard—and his brother-in-law, Charlie Mason, took their cattle into Mancos Canyon. They were sitting by their fire in the evening when out of nowhere a bunch of wild cattle appeared. By morning the visitors had gone. But when the boys counted noses, they saw that a number of their own cattle had gone off, too. The two young fellows wasted no time setting out to look for them.

It was a strange, sunless day. There was snow on the ground and the trees were covered with snow. The canyon looked like fairyland. And suddenly the boys thought they really were in fairyland.

They had climbed high up and had come on a clearing where the trees had been burned out. Standing there, they could look over the tops of the snow-laden trees down into the canyon and over to the cliff on the opposite side. And there against the cliff they saw something that made them catch their breath. They beheld shadowed caves and the walls and towers of an immense ruin.

The boys stood there and stared. They forgot about their cattle. Their only thought was to get to this dead, silent city. But how? The gray cliff cut off approach from the top. It cut off approach from the bottom. The dream city seemed to be suspended in mid-air.

Climbing, slipping, falling, somehow the boys got there. Then for hours they explored the ruins. They crawled through low doorways. They examined the great round tower in the center. They wandered about from room to room. Here was a stone axe with the handle still on it. Here were baskets, sandals with pointed toes, black and white pottery, human bones.

It was late in the afternoon when they remembered their cattle. They clambered down.

"Let's separate and go looking in different directions," Richard proposed. "I'll meet you at our camp in the morning."

Soon after that Richard was on an old dim

cattle trail he had picked up. It led over bare rocks—to a spring, he guessed. His head was down, he was looking for signs of fresh tracks. Suddenly something made him look up. There in the distance, tucked into a cliff, was another ruin! It seemed a thing enchanted. It seemed to beckon to him to come and explore.

"Tomorrow, with Charlie," Richard decided.

Next day the boys no sooner met than they were off to find Richard's ruin. He had marked the place carefully in his mind. But heavy snow had fallen in the night. It lay a foot thick on the ground. Watchful as Richard was, he missed the trail and the boys found themselves going this way and that.

All at once they stood stock still. Before them was quite a different ruin! Perched on the opposite cliff it lay—an immense dead city with a square tower five stories high.

After that day the Wetherill boys were always up and down the cliffs. That same winter John Wetherill and three of his friends climbed up with packs on their backs to the ruin of the square tower. For a month they camped in a great round underground chamber. They wandered about the 200 rooms, exploring, examining, collecting. *Cliff Palace* they called the ruin.

What had happened to its inhabitants? Where had they vanished? What had they been like?

After a while the boys felt almost as though they had known the people whose home this had been. Here were their corn, beans, squashes. Here was their turkey pen. Here were their tools made out of stone and deer bone. Here were their pottery, their baskets, scraps of their clothing, ornaments. The boys could almost see the Indians dressed in the feather blankets and strings of beads.

Where had all that life gone? The buzzards sailing lazily by could not tell the boys. The skeletons they dug up could not speak.

That was just one adventure. Every year held a new one. One day in 1891 four of the Wetherill boys—Richard, Al, John, and Clayton—set out from the ranch house. They were going to make a collection of old Indian things.

They were digging in a shallow cave in Grand Gulch, Utah when they came upon something entirely new. Here were skeletons with the flesh dried on them as on a mummy. Over the head of each was a huge basket. Beside each body was a pair of new sandals such as the boys had never seen before. The sandals had square toes.

The peculiar thing about these mummies was that the skulls were narrow. The boys had found dozens of Indian skeletons before. The skulls of all of them had been much broader. Was this a different people perhaps?

Was it also an earlier people? The boys were puzzled. They saw no sign of pottery anywhere. And yet these Indians had baskets. Was it possible that people had learned how to make baskets before they learned how to make pots? Baskets seemed so much more difficult. Had baskets really come before pots?

The boys had no answers. They were simple ranchers, they could only ask the questions. They would tell the scholars about these *Basket Makers* they had found.

Another time John Wetherill was making a collection for the World's Fair. Al and Clayton had gone along with him. They were digging in a ruin they had named *Step House*. They had already explored it before, but they knew there was much more work to be done here, especially in the cave. They had only scratched the surface. They felt sure that down under the fallen walls, down under the levels of rubbish, they would find things nobody had ever seen before.

However, as they dug, they began to wonder whether they hadn't made a mistake. They had come to the end of the rubbish. Under it there seemed to be nothing but solid dust. The dust looked as if only more of the same could lie beneath. But still John insisted on digging.

They cut through one, two, three feet of dirt. Then at last their spades struck against stone. Remains of walls appeared. Pottery appeared. They dug up piece after piece—twenty-one pieces in all. It was different from the black-and-white pottery they had found before. This was crude, rough stuff. It must have been made by people who had just learned to make pots out of clay. Were these descendants of the Basket Makers?

CHAPTER 18

Basket Makers

THE EYES OF SCHOLARS ALL OVER THE WORLD
began to turn to the American Southwest.
For here, sleeping in the cliffs and caves, lay the
Americans of long ago. The Wetherill boys had
ripped the veil from a mystery. Now a lot of questions were going to be answered.

The scholars came. Famous men from famous

museums followed in the footsteps of the Wetherill boys, digging, sorting, comparing, fitting
together. And bit by bit the jigsaw puzzle the
boys had laid bare took shape. The Anasazi came
to life.

Anasazi—the Ancient Ones. That is the name
the Navajo Indians gave to the people who lived
in this land long ago. They lumped the ancients
all together—Anasazi. But every scholar could
see that many hundreds of years must have
passed between the beginnings of one group of
Anasazi and another.

When had the Basket Makers come into the
land?

No one could say exactly. Two thousand years
before Columbus sailed, perhaps. They were
already there when the Romans conquered the
Old World. They were there when savage tribes
fought one another in the British Isles. They
were certainly there by the time Christ was
born.

The Basket Makers came into the land, a straggly looking group. They didn't look so very
different from their ancestors who had crossed
thousands of years ago into an unknown land.

They didn't have much more. They didn't know much more—you can't learn much when you are wandering around. Short, small-boned, with long heads and thin, delicate faces, they didn't look very strong. They were nearly naked. The men came carrying their tools and throwing sticks. They had no bows and arrows yet, just these atlatls to give their darts more force. The women came with babies in their arms and burden baskets on their backs. The naked children and the dogs brought up the rear.

They came. They looked upon the sunny land. They saw the shadowy caves along the cliffs, the yucca flowering in the desert. They saw the rabbits scampering. And they said: "It is a good land. It will give us all we need."

They said so only because they needed so little. For it was not really a rich and bountiful land. It was a difficult land to live in. But it didn't matter to the Basket Makers that rain fell seldom—they didn't know how to grow things yet. It didn't matter that the grass was thin—they had no animals to pasture. The shallow caves were shelter enough.

The yucca would give them fibre. They would

wrap narrow strips of rabbit fur around the yucca strings and tie the strips together in rows to make fur blankets. They would weave baskets out of yucca fibre. They would make sandals out of yucca cord. For good strong string to tie them with they would make cord out of the women's hair.

Food would be no problem. They would hunt deer and mountain sheep and mountain lions. They would make strong traps out of yucca fibre and human hair. In them they would snare rabbits and prairie dogs and gophers and badgers and field mice and birds. They would roast the meat before an open fire. They would put water into closely woven baskets and drop hot stones in and make savory cooked food out of flesh and roots and bulbs.

So the Basket Makers took a small piece of the Southwest and made it their own. They hunted and trapped and gathered food and built rude houses and lived and loved.

Sometime around the year One a wonderful thing happened to them. Traders came from the South. They brought with them a strange new food to exchange for baskets. Maize they called it. You could put the yellow seed into the ground and it would grow into a tall green plant, taller than a man. The plant would bear the seed a hundredfold. Only you had to tend the maize and drive the birds away. You could dry the seed and grind it and mix the meal with water and bake cakes on a hot stone. There was a food for you! And you could store this maize. It would keep all winter, it would keep for years.

So the Basket Makers became farmers. They grew maize—and squashes, too. They dug pits and lined them with stone and stored their maize in them.

Sometimes when their loved ones died, they would empty out a pit and bury the dead person in it. Over his head they would put a great basket. By his side they would put his best belongings—his atlatl, his snares, his digging stick, his bead and feather ornaments, perhaps his flute— and always a pair of new, square-toed sandals. Sometimes they would kill his dog and bury it with him for company in that other world. They would leave a red-painted bone for the dog, too.

For hundreds of years Basket Makers lived like this. They didn't change their ways much. They did just what their fathers and mothers had done.

Now and again they learned some brand new thing. They made clay pots and, by accident, learned to bake them in the fire. Another time they got acquainted with beans. They tamed the turkey and learned the trick of making blankets of feather cord. They made needles out of turkey bones. They dried and used its skin for cloth. They learned to use the bow and arrow.

A simple people—Basket Makers. They didn't have much. They didn't know much. But they could well be proud. They took what Nature had to offer and made it fit their human needs. They stayed in one place and built. They built the groundwork. Others would come after. Others would reach higher. They would stand on Basket Maker shoulders.

CHAPTER 19

Retreat to the Heights

Who were the people who reached above the Basket Makers?

That was something the scholars were struggling with. Anybody could see that around the year 700 something happened. People whose skulls were curiously flat behind had come to live side by side with the Basket Makers. Then

146

little by little the people with the flattened skulls took over. The normal heads got fewer and fewer. Then they simply vanished altogether.

What happened? Did the flat-heads kill off the Basket Makers? It didn't look that way. No, there they were living peacefully side by side as anybody could see. What, then, was the explanation?

Scholars said this and scholars said that. But at last the right answer came. The flat-heads weren't a new people at all. They were Basket Makers. They were Basket Makers whose mothers had somewhere picked up the trick of strapping babies to a hard cradle board. It made their heads flat behind. People had thought the fashion handsome. By and by all the Basket Makers were doing it. And at last there wasn't a normal-headed Basket Maker left.

What were the scholars to do now? They had already called the flat-headed people by a different name—Pueblos. That was the name the Spaniards had given to the Indian communities of the Southwest. The name had stuck. Both the people and their houses were still called Pueb-los.

Well, now the scholars would have to make explanations. They would have to make it clear that the Pueblos of long ago and the Basket Makers of longer ago than that were all one people. For well over two thousand years this people had lived in the little crossroads of the world where Colorado, Utah, Arizona, and New Mexico meet. Even today the blood of the Anasazi flowed in the veins of the Pueblos.

But with the head-flattening something had started among the Anasazi. Around the year 700 the people had begun to develop faster. They learned how to make better pottery, finer string sandals. They started growing cotton, making cotton blankets, making cotton clothing. They learned to make axes to chop their wood. They made hoes to cultivate their maize. They built looms to weave their cotton on. They built great round underground chambers for religious ceremonies. They started building houses with enough rooms for a whole clan of people.

But all this was just the beginning. The

148

Golden Age of the Pueblos was yet to come. It would come soon because now the groundwork was laid.

It is the year 1000. In Europe people are expecting the end of the world to come—so it has been prophesied. Instead, a new world is about to be revealed. Norsemen Leif Ericson, sailing from Norway, comes upon the western land he has been seeking. He calls it *Vineland the Good.*

He has no notion of the size of this new land. He does not know the kind of people who live in it. The Norsemen who come after him see a canoeful of Indians. They call the Indians Skraelings. The Norsemen think only savages inhabit this land. They cannot see across three thousand miles.

But three thousand miles away the Pueblos are building apartment houses of stone and wood and clay. They build them high up in caves on the cliffs or high up on top of the mesas. That's for protection.

The Pueblos are a peaceloving people, but they have warlike neighbors. Their neighbors are envious. They come raiding, come stealing their good maize and beans. They come to carry off their turquoise.

So the Pueblos retreat to the heights. They build apartment houses with hundreds of rooms —big enough to shelter a whole city. They build the houses up to five stories high. One story is set back above another so that there will be a terrace in front of each home for work and play. They put ladders on the terraces to climb in and out. When the alarm comes, they can scurry up the ladders and pull them in after themselves.

In the Chaco Canyon of New Mexico the Pueblos have built twelve great apartment houses. Some are rectangular, some are oval, some are shaped like a half moon. They are up to four stories high on three of the sides and one-storied on the fourth. Inside the walls are great open courts and underground ceremonial chambers. The houses have hundreds of rooms. One of the largest will one day—nearly a thousand years away—be called *Pueblo Bonito*. It is a whole town. It is built in the open and covers three acres of ground. It contains at least 800 rooms. It houses 1200 people. It is the largest apartment house the world will see until the year

1882 when New York will have a bigger one.

High on the cliffs of Mesa Verde the Pueblos are building apartment houses, too. One day they will be discovered by a couple of boys out looking for their cattle. *Cliff Palace* the boys will call the largest of the houses. It is a city. It shelters hundreds of farmers and their families.

For the Pueblos are really farmers now. Their life depends on what they raise. They have mastered agriculture. They no longer plant their maize a foot down so that it will reach underground water. They understand irrigation now. They have dug ditches miles long to bring water to their corn. They have built dams to catch the run-off of the heavy summer rains. They have built reservoirs.

The apartment house set in the side of the cliff has 200 rooms and twenty-one ceremonial chambers. The building is handsomely terraced. It reaches up to four stories. There are towers with doors in them but no windows. What do the farmers want with towers? Are they for defense? Are they for observation? The towers will puzzle scholars a thousand years from now.

Such buildings are built to last forever. Why

then do the Pueblos leave? Why do they abandon what they have built with so much effort?

For a long time scholars couldn't see any sufficient reason for it. They thought of enemy raids. They thought of quarrels among the Pueblos themselves. Some put it down to general restlessness. "They just got tired of living in the same place," they said.

But nobody was really satisfied until Dr. A. E. Douglass started to study tree rings. He put his finger on the main reason. Between the years 1277 and 1299 there had been a terrible drought. The drought had been so bad that trees had scarcely grown at all. The yearly rings in the ancient beams showed it clearly. All the ditches and dams and reservoirs of the Pueblos had not been sufficient to save their crops. Their corn and beans and squash had withered and died.

The Pueblos had stuck it out for a while—as long as they could. But when nearly all the corn they had saved for such a time was gone, they simply had to go away.

First one group drifted off and then another. They turned their faces to the South. They never came back. Some mingled with this tribe, some with that.

The Golden Age of the Pueblos was over. As a people the Anasazi had ceased to exist.

CHAPTER 20

Mound Builders

ALL THROUGH THE EAST, AMERICA IS COV-
ered with man-made hills—from the Mississippi
to the Appalachians, from Wisconsin to the
Gulf of Mexico. They are strewn over twenty
States. There are probably 100,000 of them.
Some are huge, covering many acres. Some are
much smaller.

154

There are mounds shaped like cones. There are mounds like pyramids with their tops cut off. Some are in the shape of flying birds, animals of various kinds, serpents, human beings. From the air they look like huge cookie cut-outs.

Some are embankments inclosing great areas. The enclosures are in the form of squares, circles, octagons, crescents—all very nearly true and perfect.

Who built these mounds? When? What for?

The pioneers pushing westward asked the Indians: "Did you build these hills?"

The Indians shook their heads. They knew nothing about the Mound Builders.

That made the hills all the more wonderful—there was a mystery about them.

Well, if the Indians didn't know who built them or why, the thing to do was to look for the answer inside. So people started to dig into the mounds. They opened up this one and that, and the more they opened, the more puzzled they became. They found things they simply couldn't explain.

Here along with human bones were pearl necklaces and copper breastplates. Here were beautiful tobacco pipes in the shape of animals and birds carved out of stone. Here were copper adze and axe blades, knives, spear points. Here were tools made of iron taken from meteorites. Here were silver and gold worked in the same way as copper.

Here was artistic pottery in a hundred different forms—some shaped like birds, some like animals, some like heads of human beings. Here was fine tanned leather. Here was cloth made out of fibre from bark and nettles and swamp milkweed and grasses. Some was interwoven with feathers and fur and hair.

What were people to think? None of the Indians who lived in the mound area could make such things. They were deer and buffalo hunters. They didn't know the use of metals. They were not artists and craftsmen.

It must be that the Mound Builders were not Indians at all. That must be the answer. The Mound Builders must have come to America from somewhere else. Maybe they were Chinese. No, more likely they were Egyptians; because didn't Egyptians build pyramids too? But maybe, again, they were the Ten Lost Tribes of Israel. Or perhaps they came from the lost Continent of Atlantis—or of Mu.

Pioneer newspapers and magazines had plenty to write about. Learned pamphlets and books appeared. Any idea seemed more likely than that the Mound Builders were Indians.

But in the end all the exciting theories had to be dropped.

"The Mound Builders were Indians," the scholars decided. "But they were very superior Indians. Compared with the Mound Builders, the Indians whom the pioneers met were savages."

"But what did your civilized Indians build the mounds for?" people wanted to know.

The scholars had been digging into the man-made hills a good long time now. They had the answer ready.

"They built them for different reasons," they said. "Some mounds—especially the cone-shaped ones—were burial mounds. They aren't any different from the thousands of mounds in the Old World. People have for ages piled up earth over their dead by way of doing them honor—a hill is a monument that lasts and lasts. As for the mounds shaped like pyramids with the tops cut off, they were platforms for buildings. Temples and other structures stood on them once. And the embankments were fortifications."

"What about the ones in the shape of animals and birds?"

About those the scholars couldn't agree. They had gone up to Wisconsin where most of the cookie cut-outs were and had studied them. They had found burials sometimes in the middle of the earth creature's head, sometimes halfway between the head and the tail, sometimes where the heart might be expected to be.

But the scholars had also gone to Adams County in Ohio and examined the Great Serpent Mound. There was no burial there. The huge earth serpent wound for a thousand feet along the edge of a high, rocky cliff by the side of a river. Its great coils measured 1,330 feet. Its triangular head rested on a sheer precipice of rock a hundred feet high. The huge jaws were open. The gap between them measured seventy-five feet. In its jaws the serpent held an oval figure like an egg. It looked as if he was about to swallow the egg. In the middle of the egg the scholars found burnt stones. That meant an altar had been there. Did the Mound Builders worship the Serpent? Did great religious ceremonies once take place here?

The scholars couldn't say. But they agreed on one thing. It had taken a lot of energy to build that serpent.

As for the work that had gone into building *all* the mounds, that was simply staggering. "How did they ever do it?" the scholars marveled.

For it is much easier to tear down a hill than it is to build one. And the men who were studying the mounds were having a hard time of it.

The Ohio State Museum, for instance, had spent three summers tearing down one single mound. They had fifteen men on the job working with picks and shovels. They had teams and scrapers. Yet it took nine months to tear the Seip Mound down. To build it up again was a much harder problem. True, this mound was bigger than average. It was 250 feet long, 150 feet wide, and thirty feet high.

But the great Cahokia Mound at East Saint Louis was at least twenty times bigger than the Seip Mound. Cahokia Mound covered sixteen acres of ground and was a hundred feet high. How long did it take the Mound Builders to heap up that pile?

The Mound Builders had no fancy steel shovels, no horses, no wagons. Every bit of earth they put into the mound had to be painfully dug with a digging stick or a stone hoe, a clamshell or the shoulder blade of a deer or elk. Every bit of earth had to be brought from somewhere else in a basket on somebody's back. Every basketful had to be carried up, up, up and emptied. And Cahokia Mound was just one mound in a group of eighty-five huge mounds.

The scholars thought about it and marveled. "It staggers the imagination," they said.

One of them sat down and actually did the arithmetic. He figured out how long it must have taken to build just the mounds and earthworks in the State of Ohio.

"With the tools and equipment the Mound

Builders had," he said, "it would have taken 1,000 men a hundred years to do it—provided they worked 300 days a year."

There was no doubt about it—the Mound Builders were workers. Between farming and building they were as busy as ants. Just the same they found time for all kinds of industries, too. They quarried flint and made it into tools and weapons. They mined copper and other metals. They didn't know how to melt the metals. But they softened them with heat and beat them thin. They sought for pearls in clams and mussels. They worked in stone and wood and clay. They spun and wove.

And still they had time left over for vanity. The Mound Builders thought a great deal about beauty. And beauty, they decided, begins at home.

So they made themselves beads. They made beads of shell and beads of bone. They made beads from teeth and beads from claws. They hammered out copper into ornaments for their ears. They made copper rings for their fingers, copper bracelets, copper anklets, copper breast-plates and head-plates. They made copper helmets with imitation antlers of wood covered with copper. They sewed silvery mica cut-outs on their garments. Whatever was colorful or bright or glittering they used to decorate themselves.

But the great favorite was pearls. The Mound Builders were mad about pearls. They wore thick ropes of fresh-water pearls around their necks. They sewed hundreds of them on their clothing. They buried thousands of them as offerings to the gods. In one Ohio mound alone 60,000 pearls were found. The Mound Builders even made artificial pearls by wrapping mica around wooden beads.

Yes, the Mound Builders thought a lot of beauty. They were willing to go halfway across the country to get materials for beauty. They trekked to the Rockies for eye teeth of the grizzly bear. They got sea shells and shark teeth and tortoise shell from the Gulf Coast. Copper from mines near Lake Superior found its way down to Georgia. Mica from the Appalachian highlands worked its way to the Mississippi.

Scholars got a new picture of young America as they dug into the mounds. In their mind's eye they could see commerce and trade busy over thousands of miles. They saw an endless exchange of things. They saw canoes filled with raw materials plying up and down the rivers. They saw traders carrying goods on their backs north and south and east and west.

One particular trade astonished the scholars more than all the rest. That was the trade in obsidian—volcanic glass. The Mound Builders had gone all the way to the Yellowstone for it. It was the nearest place obsidian could be found. Traders had carried great heavy blocks of it on their backs for miles on weary miles. They had climbed over mountains and trudged across valleys, stumbled through forests and crossed over streams with that burden.

And when they got it to its destination, what had the Mound Builders done with it? They had made ceremonial knives out of it. Wouldn't copper have done just as well? Why did they have to have obsidian? Why were they willing to go to all that trouble to have that special kind of knife for their religious ceremonies?

One of the scholars had an answer.

"The Mound Builders wanted knives of obsidian," he said, "because that's what the Indians in Mexico used for their sacrifices. Mexico with its wonderful civilization was a great shining light. The light spread very, very far. The Mound Builders caught a gleam of it as far away as Ohio. Their arts and their crafts and their religion were just a reflection of the light that was Mexico and Central America. In fact," he added, "it is even possible that the Mound Builders originally came from Middle America."

The scholars sat up when they heard that one. It was an exciting idea. It tied a lot of loose ends together. Mexico was the land where people worshiped the Feathered Serpent. Maybe that was the meaning of the Great Serpent Mound. Maybe the Mound Builders had worshiped the serpent, too. Out of one of the mounds had come pottery and shell objects with a strange rattlesnake design. The rattlesnake had feathers around its head. Was this meant to be the Feathered Serpent of Mexico?

And the platform mounds. If the Mound Builders really came from Middle America, it was there they had learned to build pyramids. For that was the ages-old custom of the peoples of Central America and Mexico. All their temples and palaces stood on great stone pyramids to give them height. Of course, the Mound Builders built their pyramids of earth. But wasn't that because they simply didn't have stone to use?

There was the copper and silver work, too. The spool-shaped ornaments of copper the Mound Builders made for their ears were exactly like those the ancient Mexicans wore. And many of the designs had a curiously "foreign" look. The human beings the Mound Builders carved and engraved were dressed in costumes that strongly reminded scholars of Mexican priests in full dress.

Some found fault with the theory. "If your Mound Builders really did come from Middle America," they said, "it must have been 'way, 'way back. For they were already building mounds in the Mississippi Valley by the year One. So they couldn't have brought the idea of obsidian knives with them. The Mexicans weren't using such knives then."

The answer to that was trade—ideas travel along the routes of trade. Mexican traders came north. "What, you don't use knives of obsidian for your ceremonies? But that's the proper thing. No other kind will do, we assure you."

If it was the proper thing, the Mound Builders would have to have it. You mustn't take chances with magic. Maybe the rains wouldn't come if you used the wrong kind of knife.

So they trekked to the Yellowstone to get obsidian.

Their coming from Middle America would tie up another loose end, too. It would explain the fortifications and why there were more of them the farther north you went in the mound area.

For if the Mound Builders really came as strangers to the land, wouldn't they have had to fight to hold it? The Indians around them were on a much lower level. Doubtless the Mound Builders civilized some of them. But many would not have wanted to learn. And as time went on, the struggle would have become harder. For the buffalo came into their lives. The buffalo was not only meat. He was a whole department store to the Indians. The buffalo was bound to lure the young away from farming. The Mound

Builders would have had to fight to hold on to their way of life. They would have had to retreat and retreat.

For a long time they held out. For well over a thousand years they lived the life of farmers, raising their maize and beans and squash and tobacco. But finally around the year 1200 they gave up. The gleam caught from the great light in Middle America died. The Mound Builders sank to the level of the peoples around them.

"Did you build these hills?" the pioneers asked the Indians.

The Indians shook their heads. Hundreds of years had passed. It might be that Mound Builder blood flowed in their veins. But they didn't know it. They knew nothing about the Mound Builders.

CHAPTER 21

What Is Long Ago?

ONCE JOHN WETHERILL BROUGHT HOME A piece of black-and-white pottery he had dug up in Mancos Canyon. He showed it to his mother.

"Don't you imagine it's very old?" he said.

His mother nodded. "It looks as if it's been in the earth these fifty years," she said.

"Fifty!" His father chuckled. "Five hundred,

more likely. Why, that pot must have been made by the Indians of long ago."

Very old . . . Long ago . . . But what is *old*? And when was *long ago*?

"Long ago," we say, "the Mound Builders lived here."

"Long ago an ice cap lay over northern United States."

"Long ago horses no bigger than foxes scampered over the West."

"Long ago there were dinosaurs in America."

"Long ago a sea rolled where the Rockies stand today."

What is *old*? And what is the meaning of *long ago*?

A thing is old only in comparison with something less old; a thing happened long ago only in comparison with something that happened more recently. We have to have a starting point, we have to have something to measure against.

Let us, then, decide on a measuring rod for *old* and *long ago*. It must be a good long one; for we are going to measure what scientists call Geological Time. We will take Man as our start-

ing point. Man's life on earth will be our measure of Time.

We will draw a line. . . .

This line is only four inches long. But on our
scale it will represent one million years. That is
as long as men have lived on earth. They were
not all men of our own kind, of course. In fact,
our own special friend, *Homo sapiens,* took up
only a small piece of the line. He dates back
only 150,000 years. So we can give him only a
little room at the end. Our measuring rod will
look like this:

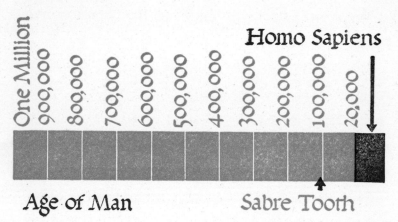

That black oblong at the end of the line is how
long men of our own kind have lived on earth.
At the point where our measuring rod says 20,-

ooo we will have to put "Minnesota Man"—the fifteen-year-old girl who drowned in the glacial lake. The scientists made a big fuss about *that* being very long ago; yet in comparison with man's stay on earth it doesn't seem so very long ago after all. Even the sabre-tooth of the Ice Age doesn't seem so very long ago.

But supposing, now, we want to show longer ago than a million years. Supposing we want to show how long men of *any* kind have lived on earth in comparison with the time when mammals took America over. How would we show that?

We would have to make our line seventy-five times as long!

Impossible on this page, of course. We shall have to start over again.

We will draw another line. But this time our line will represent not *one* but seventy-five million years.

Note, please, that we still have a little black oblong at the end. But it no longer represents the same thing. It is no longer the life of *Homo sapiens* on earth. It is the entire Age of Man—one million years. It is our whole first line shrunk to this little space. Modern man must now be represented by just a line at the very end.

But now supposing we want to see how old the Age of Man is compared to the dinosaurs. How shall we do that?

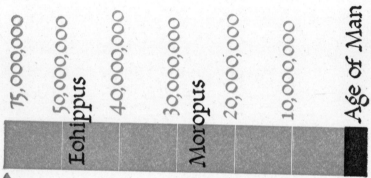

↑ *mammals take over* Age of Mammals

The Age of Reptiles—when the dinosaurs were kings—began 200 million years ago. To show how long ago that was, we would have to make our first line 200 times as long. Obviously we can't do that—a line more than sixty-six feet long would carry us off this page and out through the rear door and perhaps even to the back fence. No, we shall have to shrink our time line again. In inches it will still be the same length as before. But in time it will represent 200 million years instead of one.

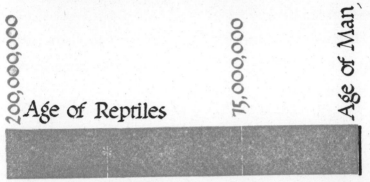

The whole Age of Man is now just a thin line at the right. *Homo sapiens* and the Ice Age animals of Rancho La Brea can't get into the picture at all. They must simply be imagined as the thinnest of thin lines at the very end.

But supposing we wanted to go still farther back. Supposing we wanted to show how long ago the rocks in the very bottom of the Grand Canyon were formed. How long a line would we need for that?

We would need a line 2,000 times as long as our first line. The four inches would have to be multiplied by 2,000. Roughly, we would need a line a tenth of a mile long!

No, we cannot draw such a line. We will have to shrink time again to fit into the four inches our page allows. How will our scale look now?

First of all we will divide our line in two. Each half will be a thousand million years long.

Geological Time Chart

The thousand million years on the left will represent a very dull period. For in all that thousand million years there was either no life at all on earth or the things that lived were such as left no fossils behind them.

Now let us divide some more. We will cut the thousand million years of living things in two.

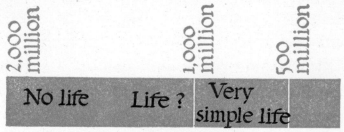

Geological Time Chart

The 500 million years blacked in will still not be very interesting—from the point of view of life. Only the very simplest kinds of plant and animal life existed then. Only here and there in the rocks of this period can a fossil be found.

But now we come to the exciting last quarter of Geological Time—the 500 million years at the right of our line. Things get really interesting from here on; for this is where the curtain goes up for our Great American Play.

Age of Invertebrates ↑

Right away we have to start dividing again. We shall have to give a little over one-fifth of that last quarter to the Age of Invertebrates— the age of creatures without a backbone. For trilobites and corals and sponges and shellfish and worms pretty much had the world to themselves then.

What next?

Next we have to make room for the fishes.

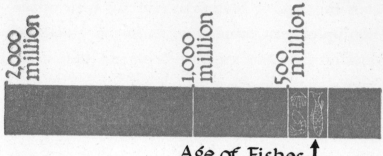

Age of Fishes ↑

There they are, taking all the leading parts. It is their act, the Age of Fishes.

And now for the great swamp forests. Their act is next. It takes a little less time than the Age of Fishes.

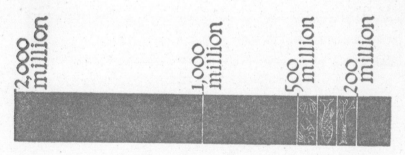

Age of Swamp Forests↑

We are up to the Age of Reptiles now. The dinosaurs are kings in America.

All the rest must happen in that little empty space at the end. That little empty space is the second line we drew. It is the Modern World. It is the Age of Mammals. In this little space Eohippus must come into being and grow and develop into the modern horse. In this space

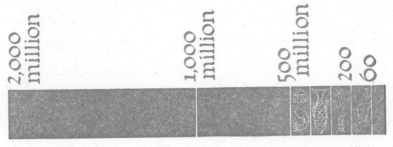

Age of Reptiles ↑

Moropus and the rhinos and the giant pig will roam along the Niobrara. In this space the Rockies must be worn down and again uplifted. The Cascade Mountains and the Sierra Nevadas must rise. Volcanoes will spout all over the West. Great lava flows will occur. Ice will come. All in this little space.

Divide that space into seventy-five parts—if you can—and the last of them will be the Age of Man.

That's where we started. That is what our measuring rod would shrink to. On our four-inch scale covering the whole 2,000 million years of Geological Time our million years would be a tiny speck—no more.

That is the meaning of *old*. When we talk of America and its story, that is the meaning of *long ago*.

Index

179

LANDMARK BOOKS

★

1. **The Voyages of Christopher Columbus**
Written and Illustrated by
ARMSTRONG SPERRY

2. **The Landing of the Pilgrims**
Written and Illustrated by
JAMES DAUGHERTY

3. **Pocahontas and Captain John Smith**
By MARIE LAWSON
Illustrator, WILLIAM SHARP

4. **Paul Revere and the Minute Men**
By DOROTHY CANFIELD FISHER
Illustrator, NORMAN PRICE

5. **Our Independence and the Constitution**
By DOROTHY CANFIELD FISHER
Illustrator, ROBERT DOREMUS

6. **The California Gold Rush**
By MAY McNEER. Illustrator, LYND WARD

7. **The Pony Express**
By SAMUEL HOPKINS ADAMS
Illustrator, LEE J. AMES

8. **Lee and Grant at Appomattox**
By MACKINLAY KANTOR
Illustrator, DONALD MCKAY

9. **The Building of the First Transcontinental Railroad**
By ADELE NATHAN
Illustrator, EDWARD A. WILSON

10. **The Wright Brothers:** *Pioneers of American Aviation*
By QUENTIN REYNOLDS
Illustrator, JACOB LANDAU

11. **Prehistoric America**
By ANNE TERRY WHITE
Illustrator, ALDREN WATSON

12. **The Vikings**
By ELIZABETH JANEWAY
Illustrator, HENRY C. PITZ

13. **The Santa Fe Trail**
By SAMUEL HOPKINS ADAMS
Illustrator, LEE J. AMES

14. **The Story of the United States Marines**
By GEORGE HUNT
Illustrator, CHARLES MAZOUJIAN

15. **The Lewis and Clark Expedition**
By RICHARD L. NEUBERGER
Illustrator, WINOLD REISS

16. **The Monitor and the Merrimac**
By FLETCHER PRATT
Illustrator, JOHN O'HARA COSGRAVE, II

17. **The Explorations of Père Marquette**
By JIM KJELGAARD
Illustrator, STEPHEN VOORHIES

18. **The Panama Canal**
By ROBERT CONSIDINE
Illustrator, FRITZ KREDEL

19. **The Pirate Lafitte and the Battle of New Orleans**
By ROBERT TALLANT
Illustrator, JOHN CHASE

20. **Custer's Last Stand**
By QUENTIN REYNOLDS
Illustrator, FREDERICK T. CHAPMAN

21. **Daniel Boone:** *The Opening of the Wilderness*
By JOHN MASON BROWN
Illustrator, LEE J. AMES

22. **Clipper Ship Days:** *The Golden Age of American Sailing Ships*
By JOHN JENNINGS
Illustrator, EDWARD A. WILSON

23. **Gettysburg**
By MACKINLAY KANTOR
Illustrator, DONALD MCKAY

24. **The Louisiana Purchase**
By ROBERT TALLANT
Illustrator, WARREN CHAPPELL

25. **Wild Bill Hickok Tames the West**
By STEWART HOLBROOK
Illustrator, ERNEST RICHARDSON

26. **Betsy Ross and the Flag**
By JANE MAYER
Illustrator, GRACE PAULL

27. **The Conquest of the North and South Poles:** *Adventures of the Peary and Byrd Expeditions*
By RUSSELL OWEN
Illustrator, LYND WARD

28. **Ben Franklin of Old Philadelphia**
By MARGARET COUSINS
Illustrator, FRITZ EICHENBERG

29. **Trappers and Traders of the Far West**
Written and Illustrated by
JAMES DAUGHERTY

30. **Mr. Bell Invents the Telephone**
By KATHERINE SHIPPEN
Illustrator, RICHARD FLOETHE